Society of St. Vincent de Paul

Rules of the Society of Saint Vincent de Paul

and indulgences granted by the sovereign pontiffs to the members and to the

benefactors of the society, and, also to its poor and the fathers and mothers of its

members, with the explanatory notes annexed

Society of St. Vincent de Paul

Rules of the Society of Saint Vincent de Paul
*and indulgences granted by the sovereign pontiffs to the members and to the benefactors of
the society, and, also to its poor and the fathers and mothers of its members, with the
explanatory notes annexed*

ISBN/EAN: 9783337300265

Printed in Europe, USA, Canada, Australia, Japan

Cover: Foto ©Andreas Hilbeck / pixelio.de

More available books at **www.hansebooks.com**

RULES

OF

THE SOCIETY OF

ST. VINCENT DE PAUL,

AND

INDULGENCES

GRANTED BY THE SOVEREIGN PONTIFFS

BOTH TO THE MEMBERS AND TO THE BENEFACTORS OF THE
SOCIETY.

WITH THE EXPLANATORY NOTES ANNEXED.

From the Manual of the Society of St. Vincent de Paul.

NEW YORK:

PRINTED FOR THE COUNCIL OF NEW YORK,

BY D. & J. SADLIER & CO., 31 BARCLAY STREET.

1869

This little book contains the Briefs of Pope Gregory XVI., the Rules of the Society of St. Vincent de Paul, with the reflections which precede them, and which should never be separated from them. It terminates with a notice of the Indulgences granted by the sovereign Pontiffs, Gregory XVI. and Pius IX., both to the members and to the benefactors of the Society.

CONTENTS.

RULES OF THE SOCIETY ST. VINCENT DE PAUL.

EXPLANATORY NOTES.

GREGORY XVI., POPE.

For the perpetual remembrance of the thing.

It becometh the Roman Pontiff to enrich, in a special
manner, with the heavenly treasures of the Church, those
pious Societies that labor with all care and zeal in the
performance of works of Christian charity. Wherefore,
having been earnestly solicited by the President and
Council General of the Society of Saint Vincent de Paul,
which was originally established in Paris, to grant to
that Society some indulgences, as well plenary as partial,
We have thought fit that their pious supplication should
be freely acceded to.

Wherefore, We mercifully grant, in the Lord, a plenary indulgence to all and every the members, whether
attached to the now instituted Council General at Paris,
of the said Society, or to particular Councils of Paris and
other cities, who, being truly penitent, shall have confessed their sins and received the Holy Communion, provided that they shall have been present at all, or at three
out of the four meetings of the Council which are holden
in the month.

Further, to all active members, as they are termed, of
the Society itself, and also the members of the Councils,
and others of whom mention has been above made, who

may have previously obtained the aforesaid indulgence,
We in like manner grant a plenary indulgence, provided
that they shall have been present at all, or at three out
of the four meetings or conferences holden in the month,
and that being truly penitent, and having confessed their
sins, they shall have received the Most Holy Sacrament
of the Eucharist. Moreover, We likewise grant the same
plenary indulgence, to be gained by all persons to be admitted into the aforesaid Society on that day, on which,
being in like manner truly penitent, and having confessed
their sins, and having received the Holy Communion,
they shall have been received into the different active
grades of aspirant member, ordinary member, member
of a particular Council, or of the Council General. Moreover, We likewise grant a plenary indulgence to all members, as well active as honorary, of the said Society, who,
on the feasts of the Immaculate Conception of the Blessed
Virgin Mary, and of Saint Vincent de Paul, and on the
second Sunday after Easter, which is the anniversary of
the translation of the relics of the same Saint Vincent;
as also on the Monday after the first Sunday of Lent, being truly penitent and having confessed their sins, shall
have received the Holy Communion at the Mass which
is celebrated on these aforesaid days for the Society, and
shall have been present at the general meeting which is
holden at these seasons. And also, in like manner, We
grant a plenary indulgence to all the members and benefactors of the Society, who, at the hour of death, being
truly penitent, and having confessed their sins, or if unable to do so, being at least contrite, shall have devoutly
invoked the name Jesus, with their lips, if able, but if
not, with their heart, and with a patient and ready spirit
shall have received death from the hand of the Lord as
the wages of sin. Moreover, We remit, according to the

usual form of the Church, seven years, and as many quarantines, of the penances enjoined on them, or otherwise in any way due by them, to all active members of the same Society, as often as, at least with a contrite heart, they shall have visited any Conference, any poor family, or the schools and workshops of the poor, or shall have performed any other good work, according to the spirit of the said Society; which partial indulgence the active members of the aforesaid Society can each gain, as often as with a contrite heart they shall attend at the Holy Sacrifice of the Mass offered up for the soul of any member, and as often as they shall have accompanied the bodies of poor persons to ecclesiastical sepulture. All and singular these indulgences and relaxations of penances We allow to be applicable, by way of suffrage, to the souls of the faithful of Christ, who shall have departed life united in charity with God. Finally, by the same, Our Apostolic authority, We give and grant all and each of the aforesaid indulgences to all other Councils and Conferences of the same Society, which, with the approbation of the Council General, are instituted, whether by the Council General itself or by the particular Councils of cities or of provinces already instituted by the Council General; also to members who live in places wherein a Conference is not yet established, if in such places they shall have performed, as far as they are able, the usual works, and shall have complied with the other conditions already prescribed. Our rule, and the rule of the Apostolical Chancery, of not granting indulgences *ad instar*, and the other Apostolical constitutions and ordinances, and all other things to the contrary hereof, notwithstanding. And We also wish that transcripts or copies, even printed ones, of these letters, bearing the signature of a person of ecclesiastical dignity, may, more-

1*

over, receive the same credit as would be given to these
letters, were they produced and shown.

Given at Rome, at St. Peter's, under the Fisherman's
Ring, the 10th day of January, 1845, in the fourteenth
year of our Pontificate.

(Place of ✠ the Seal.)

A. CARD. LAMBRUSCHINI.

Approved as a faithful translation of the Brief of his
Holiness, Gregory XVI.—New York, August 11, 1848.

✠ JOHN, Bishop of New York.

(*Seal.*)

FURTHER BRIEF OF HIS HOLINESS POPE GREGORY XVI.
TO THE COUNCIL GENERAL OF THE SOCIETY OF ST.
VINCENT DE PAUL.

GREGORY XVI, POPE.

For the perpetual remembrance of the thing.

WHEREAS the Society instituted under the auspices and
name of St. Vincent de Paul, and devoted to the performance of works of Christian charity, to Our knowledge conduces in an eminent degree to the good of religion and
the advantage of the faithful; We, in order that it may
from day to day receive fresh increase, have thought fit
that out of the celestial treasures of the Church all those
should be enriched who shall have contributed their exertions and means in aid of this Society, so that this their
zeal may become more and more ardent by the holding
forth of spiritual favors. Wherefore, We mercifully grant,
in the Lord, a plenary indulgence once in the month, to
all and singular the faithful of Christ of either sex, who
being truly penitent and having confessed their sins, and
received the Holy Communion, transmit a fixed and constant eleemosynary donation to the Council General

Moreover, We grant an indulgence of seven years, and of as many quarantines once in the month, to all Christ's faithful of either sex, who shall transmit a fixed and constant eleemosynary donation of this kind to the particular Councils of provinces or cities instituted by the Council General. Moreover, We grant an indulgence of one year, to be gained likewise, once in the month, to Christ's faithful of either sex, who by writing, or in any other way, engage to contribute any fixed and constant eleemosynary donation to Conferences approved of either by the Council General, or by the particular Councils delegated for this purpose. Finally, We grant an indulgence of seven years, and of as many quarantines, to all and singular the faithful of Christ of either sex, to be gained once in the month on those days, to wit, on which they shall have collected by questing, a pecuniary alms for the Council General, or particular Councils. Our rule, and the rule of the Apostolical Chancery, of not granting indulgences *ad instar*, and the other Apostolical constitutions and ordinances, and all other things to the contrary hereof, notwithstanding. And We also wish that transcripts or copies, even printed ones, of these letters, bearing the signature of a person of ecclesiastical dignity, may, moreover, receive the same credit as would be given to these letters, were they produced and shown.

Given at Rome, at St. Mary Major's, under the Fisherman's Ring, the 12th August, 1845, in the fifteenth year of our Pontificate.

(Place of ✠ the Seal.)

    A. CARD. LAMBRUSCHINI, Bishop of Sabine.

Approved as a faithful translation of the Brief of his Holiness, Gregory XVI.—New York, August 11, 1848.

    ✠ JOHN, Bishop of New York.

(*Seal.*)

The Right Rev. Bishop of New York has been pleased to convey his approbation of the Society in the following letter :

It is with sincere pleasure, that we give our hearty approval to the Society of St. Vincent de Paul, established in New York, which cannot fail to be of the greatest advantage to those who compose it as members, and to the community at large.

This Society has been most solemnly approved by the Holy See, and many spiritual privileges conferred by our Holy Father upon its members.

It is now widely extended throughout Catholic Europe, and its progress has been marked by many blessings, of which rich and poor have been equally partakers. We should be rejoiced to see it extended to every parish and congregation in the diocese.

Given at New York, this 11th day of August, A. D. 1848.

✠ JOHN, Bishop of New York.

(*Seal.*)

RULES

The Society of St. Vincent de Paul.

First published at Paris, in December, 1835.

WE are now entering upon that formal organization we have long wished for. It has been
delayed, for our association has already existed
some years. But were we not bound to ascertain that God wished that it should continue, before determining the form which it should assume? Was it not necessary, that it should be
well established,—that it should know what
Heaven required of it,—that it should judge
what it could do by what it had done, before
framing its rules and prescribing its duties?
Now we have only to embody, as it were, in
Regulations, usages already fo.lowed and loved;

—and this is a guarantee that our rules will be well received by all, and will not be forgotten.

Our little association for a time bore the name of *Conference of Charity of St. Vincent de Paul,* because this was the name under which it was commenced, and in order that we might not forget the circumstances of its origin, which no one in particular can attribute to himself. Some among us, whilst devoting ourselves to the defence of the dogmas of religion, in the then very stormy discussions of literary societies, thought that it was not enough to speak; but that we should also act: hence came the works of charity to which they devoted themselves—hence the *Conference of Charity.*

Having become numerous, and being obliged to divide into sections,—moreover, many of us desiring to meet together in other towns, where we were to reside thenceforth, the name of *Conference* has continued to be applied to each of those sections, all of which are comprised under the common denomination of the *Society of St. Vincent de Paul.*

We must ever avoid giving to our undertaking the name of any particular member, whatever may have been his individual services, or of the places in which we assemble, for fear we may ac custom ourselves to look upon it as the work of man. Christian works belong to God alone, the sole Author of all good.

Our association originated in religious motives: we must, therefore, look for the rules of our conduct nowhere but in the spirit of religion—in the examples and words of our Saviour—in the instructions of the Church—in the lives of the Saints. Such are the reasons why we are placed under the patronage of the Blessed and Immaculate Virgin and of St. Vincent de Paul, to whom we owe peculiar devotion, whose footsteps we must sedulously endeavor to follow.

It pleased Jesus Christ first to practise that which afterwards He was to teach mankind; *cœpit facere et docere.* We are desirous of imitating that Divine Model so far as our weakness will allow.

The object, then, of this *Conference* is, firstly, to sustain its members, by mutual example, in the practice of a Christian life; secondly, to visit the poor at their dwellings, to carry them succor in kind, to afford them, also, religious consolations, remembering these words of our Master: "Not in bread alone doth man live, but in every word that proceedeth from the mouth of God;" (Deut. viii. 3; Matt. iv. 4.) thirdly, to apply ourselves, according to our abilities and the time which we can spare, to the elementary and Christian instruction of poor children, whether free or imprisoned, seeing that what we may do for the least among our brethren, Jesus Christ has promised that He will accept as done to Himself; fourthly, to distribute moral and religious books; fifthly, to be willing to undertake any other sort of charitable work to which our resources may be adequate, and which will not oppose the chief end of the Society, and for which it may demand our co-operation upon the proposition of its directing members.

This Society of Charity is composed of active members, and of others who cannot devote themselves to the works in which it is engaged. The members of this latter class assist the former by their efforts and by their influence : by their offerings and their prayers they supply the absence of that actual co-operation which they are necessitated to forego.

The Society should endeavor to attain and practise every virtue; there are, however, some virtues which are more essentially necessary to its members, for the due discharge of the charitable duties to which they devote themselves. Among these are self-denial, Christian prudence,

the active love of our neighbor, zeal for the salvation of souls, meekness in heart and word, and
above all, the spirit of fraternal charity. They
ought, therefore, to meditate on the maxims of
the Gospel which recommend these virtues, and
should make them the rule of their lives. It is
for this purpose that those maxims are here detailed, and a development given to them applica
ble to our work.

1. By *self-denial* we should understand the sur-
rendering of our own opinion, without which sur-
render no association is durable. The man who is
in love with his own ideas will disdain the opinion of others; the contempt of his brothers, far
from uniting, engenders division. We should,
therefore, willingly acquiesce in the judgment of
others, and should not feel annoyed if our own
propositions be not accepted by them. Our mutual good-will should proceed from the heart, and
should be without bounds. We should equally
avoid all spirit of contention with the poor, and
we must not consider ourselves offended if they
should not yield implicitly to our advice; we
must not attempt to make them receive it as
from authority and by command—we should
content ourselves with proposing what is good,
and zealously exhorting to its practice, leaving

2

to God the care of making our words bear fruit, if such should be His will.

2. *Christian Prudence.* — Among the poor, there are some who have the happiness to be good Christians; others are careless, and some, perhaps, impious. We ought not to repulse them, even in this latter case; our language ought to be applicable to the dispositions of those whom we address, remembering that Jesus Christ recommended His disciples to unite the wisdom of the serpent to the simplicity of the dove. Bounty opens the heart to confidence, and it is by charitable gifts that we prepare the way for spiritual benefits. St. Vincent de Paul often recommended not to try the latter until the former had been freely bestowed. Now the poor are of either sex. As the *Society of Charity* is chiefly composed of young men, they should never forget that their mission is not to such of the other sex as are young, lest they should meet with their own destruction, whilst desiring to promote the salvation of others; moreover, it is necessary to shun even the appearance of evil, and all which might scandalize the weak.

3. *Love of our neighbor, and zeal for the salvation of souls.*—This is the very essence of the *Conference of Charity.* He who is not animated

by this twofold sentiment, which with the Christian forms but one feeling, shculd not become a member. We must never murmur at the labors, the fatigues, nor even at the repulses to which the exercise of charity may subject us. We expose ourselves to all these things, in associating for the service of our neighbor. Neither should we regret the pecuniary sacrifices that we may make to our work, esteeming ourselves happy in offering something to Jesus Christ in the persons of the poor, and in being able to carry some relief to His suffering members. We should make these sacrifices with an entire absence of personal feeling, and not conceive that the poor whom we have adopted, should be more privileged than those adopted by others, merely because we may presume that we have contributed to the common fund a larger proportion than they.

4. Our Divine Model was meek and humble of heart; "Learn of Me, because I am meek and humble of heart," St. Matt. xi. 29; and our patron, St. Vincent de Paul, prized nothing so highly as *meekness* and *humility*, which are inseparable. We should be kind and obliging to one another, and we should be equally so to the poor whom we visit. We can have no power over the mind, except through meekness. "Blessed are

the meek for they shall possess the land." St.
Matt. v. 4. The spirit of humility and meekness
is more particularly necessary in giving advice,
and in exhorting others to fly from evil and to
practise virtue. Without gentleness, zeal for the
salvation of souls is a ship without sails.

5. It is the *spirit of brotherly love* which will
insure our *Society of Charity* becoming beneficial
to its members and edifying to others. Faithful to the maxims of our divine Master and His
beloved disciple, let us love one another. We
should love one another now and ever, far and
near, from one Conference to another, from town
to town, from clime to clime. This love will
render us able to bear with one another's failings.
We shall never give credence to an evil report
of a brother but with sorrow; and when we cannot reject the evidence of facts, even then, in order to conform ourselves to the will of Him who
has confided to each one the care of his neighbor.
"To every one hath God given commandment concerning his neighbor," Eccles. xvii. 12; then,
in a spirit of charity, and with all the earnest-
ness of sincere friendship, we will ourselves counsel our falling, or fallen brother, or cause advice
to be conveyed to him; we will endeavor to
strengthen him in virtue, or raise him from his

fall. If any member of the Conference should become ill, his brethren will visit him, will tend him, if it be necessary, will assuage the irksomeness of his convalescence; if his malady be dangerous, they should take the utmost care that he receive the Sacraments. In a word, the troubles and the joys of each of us shall be shared by all, in accordance with the advice of the apostle, who tells us to weep with those who weep, and rejoice with those who rejoice.

The unity of the Society of St. Vincent de Paul will be cited as a model of Christian friendship, of a friendship stronger than death, for we will often remember in our prayers to God the brothers who have been taken from us.

This sentiment, which, with us, will make of all our hearts one heart, of all our souls one soul.—*Cor unum, et anima una,*—will endear to each of us our fraternal association; we shall bless it for the good, however trivial, it enables us to perform. We shall love this brotherhood with tenderness, and even with a greater affection than any other similar work; not because of its excellence, or from pride, but as dutiful children love a poor and deformed mother more than all other women, however remarkable they may be for their riches and for their attractions.

2*

Some other consequences of the foregoing max-ims:—

One of the vices most opposed to charity and Christian humility is envy. We should avoid it, not only amongst ourselves, but also in reference to other societies, whose object, like our own, is to succor our neighbor. We should ardently de-sire, and behold with pleasure, their prosperity, and the good they accomplish; we should rejoice if fresh brethren join us, if existing societies should unite themselves to ours, since greater good would spring from the union; but we should see without jealousy our Christian friends devoting themselves to other good works, and other socie-ties doing God's work in their own manner, and independently of us. We should have but one desire,—to see every one devote himself to do good, and to succor those who suffer: *Quis tri-buat ut omnis populus prophetet?* Nay more, although we may be fonder of our little associa-tion, we will always consider it as less excellent than others; we will regard it, as in fact it is, but as a work formed nobody knows by whom, nor how,—born yesterday, and which may die to-morrow. The same spirit should ever induce us individually to wish the offices of the Society confided to others rather than to ourselves.

We should always remember that we are only laymen, and for the most part young men, without any mission to teach others. For this, and every other reason, we will pay the utmost deference to the counsels which may be given to us by the Society or its heads; we must above all, follow with docility the directions which our ecclesiastical superiors may think proper to give us. St. Vincent de Paul wished that his disciples should not undertake any good work without having first secured the assent and received the benediction of the local pastors. In like manner, we must refer all matters appertaining to ecclesiastical jurisdiction to the director of the Society, considering as an evil any good that we could effect, contrary to his authority. We will extend, to a certain degree, this deference to the Sisters of Charity, or even to laymen who may have offices of charity to perform towards those whom we also desire to succor, esteeming it an honor to be considered the least among our brethren, and to be no more than servants and instruments of others in reference to the poor. Lastly, among ourselves the younger should defer to the elder, and the newly-admitted members to those who are of longer standing.

We are the dispensers of the gifts of God, Who

is the common Father of mankind, and makes His sun to shine upon all. Our love of our neighbor, then, should be without respect of persons. The title of the poor to our commiseration is their poverty itself. We are not to inquire whether they belong to any party, or sect, in particular. Jesus Christ came to redeem and save all men, the Greeks as well as Jews, barbarians as well as Romans. We will not discriminate more than did He, between those whom suffering and misery have visited. Nevertheless, St. Paul recommends to Christians to assist, in the *first* place, their brethren in the faith: *ad domesticos fidei.* We therefore should testify a special interest in those poor, who have the happiness of being good Christians, and who honor that title by the virtues, the practice of which religion inculcates.

The spirit of charity, together with Christian prudence, will further induce us to banish political discussions forever from our meetings, as well general as ordinary. St. Vincent de Paul would not allow his ecclesiastics even to converse upon those differences which arm princes against each other, or upon the motives of rivalry which estrange nations. With more reason, those who wish to be of one mind, and to exercise a min-

Istry of charity, should abstain from being in-
flamed by political leanings which array parties
in opposition, and from starting, amongst themselves, those irritating questions which divide
mankind. Our Society is all charity: politics
are wholly foreign to it.

Another efficacious means of maintaining unity
amongst us, and of cementing the Christian friendship of which it is the foundation and the charm,
is to present for admission into the Society only
such candidates as are worthy of the confidence
and affection of our brothers. It might be an
advantage for some persons to participate in our
charitable work; but, perhaps, it might not be
an advantage for the Society to count them
amongst its members. Previous, therefore, to
the enrolment of any friend into our ranks, we
should carefully inquire whether he be calculated
to draw closer those ties which bind us to each
other; whether the amenity of his disposition
and his Christian demeanor will enhance the
value of the small relief which he will be commissioned to carry to the distressed; whether
the firmness of his character authorizes us to
hope that he will persevere in his generous re-
solutions.

The choice of new members is of the utmost

importance. Defections we have already nad to lament—others are going on even now: there will be some always :—such is human weakness. Yet the Society will inspire some confidence,— will be efficient for some good, only so far as its members will prove its worth by their entire conduct, and particularly by their perseverance in the acts of charity to which they devote themselves.

Another point no less worthy of our consideration is, the discretion which should accompany zeal for the salvation of souls. All fervor is not holy nor accepted by God. All times are not suitable for instilling new and Christian teaching into the heart. We must know how to wait for God's own time, and to be patient as He is. Often we must wait entire weeks before we are able to inculcate, with effect, even one moral and edifying maxim. Above all, we must never be importunate upon this point. We are not commissioned to perform the good which it is out of our power to effect. On the other hand, the apparently trifling results of our mission must not discourage us. Perhaps the Almighty wills not that we ourselves should witness the happy results which our efforts and our sacrifices may at last produce. Our charity would be less meri torious, and might expose us to vainglory, if we saw it always crowned with success.

Christian prudence should never abandon us in the ministrations which we fulfil towards the poor. Unfortunately, and especially in large towns, the poor sometimes try to conceal such resources as they may have, and thus draw to themselves that sympathy and those alms which should be shared with others. Therefore, without arming ourselves with a distrust which might be unjust towards them, we must be circumspect. It is not wise to rely too implicitly upon their first statements.

It will, therefore, be a duty to ascertain their real condition from the clergy, or from those persons most able to afford us information upon the subject. We must be provident for the poor, who are seldom provident for themselves. If we wish to become their true benefactors, we should impress upon them that an existence sustained by the aid of charity is very precarious— we should induce them to exert themselves to earn their own livelihood—we should point out to them sources of employment, and we should assist them to obtain it. If they are sick or unable to work, we should second their endeavor

to obtain admission to the asylums established
for the aged, the infirm, the sick.

In conclusion, we must never be ashamed of
the smallness of our alms. That which is small
in the estimation of the rich, is great in the eyes
of those who possess nothing. The smallness of
our alms is one of the conditions of our existence.
We have no other ordinary resources than our
own voluntary offerings; these will not be sufficient for considerable works of charity; but our
tender interest—our very manner, will give to
our alms a value which they do not possess in
themselves.

We must now lay down some rules, and mention some practices we have been in the habit
of following; other customs will, doubtless, be
hereafter added—other rules will become necessary; but the existing rules, and the customs in
use, will suffice to guide our future progress.

•

RULES.

GENERAL REGULATIONS.

ARTICLE 1. All Christian young men who desire to unite in a communion of prayers and a participation of the same works of charity, may become members of the Society of Saint Vincent de Paul, wherever they may happen to reside.

ART. 2. No work of charity should be regarded as foreign to the Society, although its special object is to visit poor families. Thus, its members are expected to embrace every opportunity of affording consolation to the sick and to prisoners, of instructing poor, unprotected, or imprisoned children, and of procuring the succors of religion for those who need them, at the hour of death.

ART. 3. When several members of the Society are found in any locality, they meet to encourage each other in the practice of virtue. This meeting is called a *Conference*, the name originally given to the Society itself.

ART. 4. Should several Conferences be formed

3

in the same town, each takes the name of the parish where its members meet, and the several Conferences are united by a *Particular Council*, which takes the name of the town itself.

ART. 5. All the Conferences of the Society are united by a Council-General.

———◆———

CHAPTER I.

THE CONFERENCES.

ARTICLE 6. The Conferences meet upon such days and at such hours as they themselves may appoint.

ART. 7. The Conferences should endeavor to carry on a correspondence with each other for their mutual edification and support,—and that they may be able, whenever necessary, to recommend to the kind offices of each other, either the members themselves of the Society, or other young men, or the poor families who change their places of abode.

§ 1. *Organization of Conferences.*

ART. 8. The business of each Conference ministered by a President, a Spiritual D' one or more Vice-Presidents, a Secretary, and a Treasurer, who constitute the *Council* of the Conference. There may be also in each Conference, if necessary, a Librarian, a Keeper of the Clothes-Room, or other officers.

ART. 9. The President is elected by the Conference. The other officers are appointed by the President, with the advice of his Council. However, as is said farther on, in the town where there is a Council of Direction, the Presidents, Vice-Presidents, and other officers of the Conferences, are appointed by the President of the Council. The Spiritual Director is always appointed by the Bishop or Archbishop of the Diocese.

ART. 10. The President directs the business of the Conference, receives and submits propositions, calls meetings, if necessary, and watches over the execution of the rules and the decisions of the Society. In case of absence, he entrusts his duties to a Vice-President.

ART. 11. The Secretary prepares the minutes of the meetings. He keeps a registry of the names, professions, and residences of the members, of the dates of their admission, and the names of those by whom they were proposed. He keeps an exact account of all the families visited. He makes diligent inquiry concerning

those recommended for relief, so that the Conference may not, if possible, visit any family which
is not worthy of its sympathy and support. He
notes any changes that occur in the families visited, or in the members who visit them.

ART. 12. The Treasurer has the care of the
funds, and takes at each meeting an exact account
of the receipts and disbursements.

ART. 13. The Librarian collects instructive
books adapted to the capacity of the persons relieved by the Conference, and keeps an account
of all books lent or bestowed.

ART. 14. The keeper of the wardrobe collects
the clothes for the poor, and keeps a regular account of them.

§ 2.   *Order of the Meetings.*

ART. 15. The Spiritual Director, or in his absence the President, opens each meeting with the
prayer *Veni Sancte Spiritus*, followed by the
Prayer, with the *Ave Maria*, and *Invocation of
St. Vincent de Paul.* A portion of some pious
book selected by the Spiritual Director or President is then read. Each member is called upon
in turn to perform this duty. The duty of prayer
and pious reading should be discharged with the
most serious attention; the spiritual good of the

members being as much the object of the Society as the relief of the poor.

ART. 16. The Secretary reads the minutes of the preceding meeting. Each member is at liberty to make observations upon them.

ART. 17. If there be occasion, the President announces the admission of candidates proposed at the preceding meeting, and invites their proposers to inform them of it.

ART. 18. The President then announces the names of new candidates, should any such have been presented. Members who have any observations to make in relation to the candidates, communicate such in writing, or verbally, to the President, in the interval between the meeting at which the names are announced, and that which follows next after. If no observations have been made, the admission of the member proposed takes place at the latter meeting. Each member should be careful not to introduce into the Society any one who will not edify his fellow members, or be edified by them, and who will not endeavor to love his colleagues and the poor as brothers.

ART. 19. The Treasurer announces the state of the funds and the amount of the collection made at the close of the preceding meeting, so that each

3*

member may proportion his demands for relief to the resources of the Conference.

ART. 20. Tickets available for relief in kind, and which vary according to the requirements of the poor, are then distributed. Each member is called upon in his turn by the President, and mentions aloud what he applies for, and for how many families. He gives, when called upon to do so, detailed information about these families. The relief should be punctually given to the poor at their residences, before the next meeting. But the members administering it may use their own discretion, both as to the precise time, number, and manner of their charitable visits, and also as to the best means of introducing into these families the love of religion and the practice of their duties. Should a member ask for any rules to guide his conduct, or for advice in difficult cases, he is heard with attention and kindness, and receives from the President and every other member such replies as their experience and charity suggests.

ART. 21. If relief in money, clothes, or books be applied for, the grounds of such application should be fully explained, and the Conference votes. Should the case of distress be such that a grant of money is indispensable, and that relief in kind will not answer instead, the members receiving the money must take special care to watch diligently over the use made thereof.

ART. 22. After the allocation of the different sorts of relief, the members deliberate on the disposal of any situations they may be able to procure for the poor, on the plans for the relief of the distressed, and on the families to be visited by new members, or by those who wish to visit more. No family can be admitted on the relief roll of the Society without a previous statement of its wants, made either by the Secretary, or by such other member as may have been appointed by the President to collect information. Before the Conference decides, every member has full liberty to make any remarks upon the case he may think useful.

ART. 23. Members leaving for a time, or forever, the place where the Conference is, give notice to the President, who confides to others the duties with which such members were charged.

ART. 24. The Conference then considers any observations that may be made with a view to its interests, its increase, and the best use of its funds.

ART. 25. At the close of the meeting, and before the prayer, the Treasure makes the collec-

tion, to which each member contributes an offering proportioned to his means, but always in
secret. Those who cannot spare time for the
service of the poor, try to increase the amount
of their pecuniary contributions. The collection
is intended for the use of the families visited, but
the members should not neglect any other means
that may present themselves of increasing the
funds of the Conference.

ART. 26. The meeting closes with *the prayer
to Saint Vincent de Paul,* and the prayers *Pro
benefactoribus,* and *Sub tuum præsidium.*

CHAPTER II.

PARTICULAR COUNCILS.

ARTICLE 27. The *Particular Council* of a town
is composed of a President, a Spiritual Director,
Vice-President, Secretary, and Treasurer, of all
the Presidents, Spiritual Directors, and Vice-
Presidents of the Conferences of the town, and
of the Presidents, Spiritual Directors, and Vice-
Presidents of Special Works in which all are interested.

ART. 28. The *Particular Council* is charged

witn those works and important measures which interest all the Conferences of the town.

ART. 29. It decides on the allocation of the common fund. This fund is maintained by all donations not made expressly to any of the Conferences; collections made at the general meetings of the town, and by the contributions which the Presidents bring to the Council in the name of of their respective Conferences. This fund is intended to meet the expenses of the special works of the town, and to sustain the poorer Conferences.

ART. 30. The President, Spiritual Director, Vice-President, Secretary, and Treasurer, constitute the ordinary Council, to which belongs the direction of the ordinary business.

ART. 31. The President is appointed by the Council, with the advice of the Conferences. On the first occasion, he is appointed by the united Conferences. The President appoints the Presidents and the Vice-Presidents of Conferences and of Special Works, as well as the Vice-President, the Secretary, and the Treasurer of the Particular Council, taking the advice of his Council upon all these appointments.

ART. 32. The President of the Particular Council directs its proceedings, receives and submits

propositions, and calls meetings when necessary.
He presides at the general meetings of the district.

ART. 33. The Secretary prepares the minutes
of the meetings of the Council. He keeps a register of the names, Christian names, professions,
and residences of the members of all the Conferences of the town, with the dates of their admission, and the names of their proposers. He
also registers the native places of those who have
not a fixed domicile in the town.

ART. 34. The Treasurer has charge of the common fund of the town.

ART. 35. The Conferences are represented in
the Particular Council by their Presidents and
Vice-Presidents. The President, Spiritual Directors and Vice-Presidents of *Special Works* appear
there to watch over the interests of these works.
Each makes reports when invited to do so by the
President of the Council.

————◆————

CHAPTER III.

THE COUNCIL-GENERAL.

ARTICLE 36. The Council-General is composed
of a President, Vice-President, Secretary, Treasurer, and of several Councillors.

•

ART. 37. The Council-General is tne bond of all the Conferences—it maintains the unity of the Society. It labors for whatever can promote its prosperity. In this respect it adopts the course which it judges most useful.

ART. 38. It decides upon the allocation of the central fund. This fund is maintained by donations made to the Society, by collections made at the general meetings of the Society, and by contributions from the Conferences and Councils towards the general expenses of the Society.

ART. 39. The members of the Council-General are nominated by the President, with the advice of the Council.

ART. 40. When a President-General of the Society is to be nominated, the Council-General is convened by the Vice-President. This meeting is preparatory, its sole business being to deliberate as to the person who may be considered eligible for the office. If the former President be living, he is requested to designate some person whom he thinks it would be proper to select.

When the Council has deliberated upon one or more names, it adjourns for two months. In the interval, the proceedings of this preparatory meeting are made known to the Presidents of the Particular Councils, who consult their colleagues, and to the Presidents of the Conferences, who consult their respective Councils, or even the Conferences over which they preside; all the Presidents transmit their opinions to the Council-General, and according to these opinions the Council-General makes the election; an exact minute of which is recorded. While the election is pending, all the members of the Society offer up, either in private or in their meetings, as a special prayer to God, the *Veni Creator*, that His Spirit may enlighten them in the choice they are about to make.

ART. 41. The President-General convokes extraordinary meetings, and presides both in the Council-General and in all general meetings.

ART. 42. The Secretary-General keeps a register of the names, Christian names, professions, residences, and dates, of admission of the members; also of the officers of the Councils or Conferences, and of the places, days, and hours of their meetings. He prepares the minutes of the meetings of the Council-General, and of general meetings. He draws up an annual report on the state of the works of the Society. He is charged with the general correspondence with the Presidents or Secretaries of the several Councils or Conferences. He keeps the archives of the Society.

Art. 43. The Treasurer-General has charge of the funds. He keeps a regular account of the receipts and disbursements, and submits his accounts to the Council-General.

Art. 44. If the President-General himself cannot preside at the Council of Paris, he appoints a member of the Council-General to do so. He also, on the recommendation of the Secretary-General, appoints several members of the Council-General to the office of Vice-Secretaries.

CHAPTER IV.

GENERAL MEETINGS.

Article 45. General meetings are held every year, on the 8th of December, the feast of the Immaculate Conception of the Blessed Virgin; on the first Sunday of Lent; on the Sunday of the Good Shepherd (the anniversary of the translation of the relics of Saint Vincent de Paul;) and on the 19th of July, the feast of this our patron Saint. The President is empowered, moreover, to call extraordinary general meetings.

Art. 46. The general meetings, like the Conferences, open with prayer and pious reading.

Art. 47. The Secretary having first read the

4

minutes of the preceding meeting, calls aloud the members admitted into the different Conferences since the last general meeting, and whose names have been remitted to him for this purpose by the different Presidents. These members rise— the Secretary presents them to the Society and to the President, who addresses them in a few words.

ART. 48. The Presidents of Conferences report on the state of their Conferences. A summary abstract of each report, containing the changes of members and of poor families, the total receipts, with the amount and items of the expenditure, is deposited in the hands of the Secretary.

ART. 49. The Secretary then reads letters from those Conferences which have not been able to send a representative to the meeting. He also reads extracts of any other letters which may interest the Society.

ART. 50. The President then announces the measures taken by the Council of Direction for the good of the Society, and, if necessary, solicits the advice of the meeting.

ART. 51. The President, or any member of the Society invited by him, addresses the meeting in a few words of Christian and charitable exhortation. The Society considers itself fortunate when persons eminent for their character, their virtue, and their knowledge, are good enough to be present upon the invitation of the President at the general meeting, and to close it with some edifying remarks.

ART. 52. After the collection and usual prayers, the meeting closes.

CHAPTER V.

THE DIFFERENT MEMBERS OF THE SOCIETY.

ARTICLE 53. Besides its active members, the Society has corresponding members, honorary members, and subscribers.

ART. 54. A member changing his residence and going to a place where there is no Conference of Saint Vincent de Paul, does not thereby cease to belong to the Society;—he becomes a *corresponding member;* he puts himself in communication with the Conference or Conferences of the town of the diocese nearest to his residence, and corresponds with the Secretary of the Council or of the Conference of that town. Should there be no Conference in his diocese, he corresponds with the Secretary-General. He receives every year a report on the works of the Society, and main-

tains with it a communion both of prayers and
good works, by doing whatever works of charity
he can, and by advancing the interests of the Society whenever he has an opportunity.

ART. 55. Honorary members do not assist at
the ordinary meetings of the Conferences. They
are invited, like the ordinary members, to all
other meetings. They are to send every year a
special offering to the Treasurer of the Council or
Conference of their town. The forms of admission are the same for ordinary and honorary
members; when several Conferences are established in a town, honorary members are admitted
by the Particular Council.

ART. 56. Every Conference may have, moreover, simple subscribers—these are not members
of the Society, but are entitled as benefactors to
its prayers.

CHAPTER VI.

THE FESTIVALS OF THE SOCIETY.

ARTICLE 57. The Society celebrates the Feast
of the Immaculate Conception of the Blessed
Virgin, and the Feast of St. Vincent de Paul, its
Patron. The Conferences assists in a body at
mass, on the 8th of December and 19th of July,

and also on the anniversary of the translation of the relics of St. Vincent de Paul. On these days the members pray for the prosperity of the Catholic Church, for the increase of charity amongst men, and to draw down the blessings of God on the work in which they are associated. Should any member be absent from the locality, or otherwise prevented from attending, he assists in spirit at least with his brethren, and prays for them as they pray for him.

ART. 58. The day after the general meeting in Lent, all the members of the Society assist in a body at the *Requiem* Mass, which is offered in the town for the repose of the souls of the deceased members of the Society.

OBSERVATION.

ART. 59. None of the preceding rules impose an obligation of conscience, but the Society relies for their fulfilment on the zeal of its members, and their love of God and of their neighbor.

———◆———

It is by following the above rules, which down to the present moment were mere customs, that the young Christian associates of the Society of

4*

St. Vincent de Paul, have hitherto endeavored to
attain the double end:—

Of learning to know and love each other;

Of learning to know, love, and serve the poor
of Jesus Christ.

The establishment of separate Conferences has
not proved an obstacle to the accomplishment of
this double end: Christian intimacy has grown
even stronger between the members of the same
section than was possible between the members
of the whole Society.   There is no solitude like
that of a crowd, and large assemblies are very
like the multitude we see passing and bustling
along, but which excites no interest in our breast,
nor feels any for us.   Besides, from time to time
we correspond with distant Conferences.   Those
belonging to the same town meet together; and
such meetings and letters make our ties the
stronger.   Neither is distance nor any other obstacle insurmountable for friendship, grounded
upon community of prayer and charitable deeds.

Be of good courage, therefore; whether together or separate, far or near, let us love each
other, let us love and serve the poor.   Let us
love that little Society which made us known to
one another, which placed us in the path of a
more Christian and charitable life.   Let us love

our customs, our rules: by adhering strictly
to them, we shall be most certainly kept in the
true path, as they will keep up our work. "A
great deal of evil is done," said a holy priest to
another charitable association; "let us do a little
good." Oh! how delightful it will be one day
to find that we have not allowed the days of our
youth to glide away uselessly! Youth is a field
that requires a reaper. Let us not run through
it in haste, and without regard to futurity; let us
look around us; let us carefully glean every one
of the ears that lie at our feet; let us do a little
good, for that good is a sheaf of provision for
life;—that good will be fruitful for us in the
eyes of the Lord.

REGULATIONS
FOR THE UPPER COUNCILS.
[Drawn up by the General Council, on the 1st of April, 1850.]

ARTICLE 1. When the Conferences of a more
extensive circumscription than that of a Particular Council, desire to be united by a Council, an
Upper Council may be constituted for this purpose, conformably to the terms of the Brief of

our Holy Father, Pope Gregory XVI., dated January the 10th, 1845. This Council is named after the circumscription for which it is established, and which is determined by the Council-General; its seat is fixed by the Council-General.

This Council, within its circumscription, is the representative of the General Council, which forms the centre of the whole Brotherhood, and it governs all the Councils and Conferences already established, or which may be established there. Its object is to preserve the unity and spirit of the Brotherhood there; it forms the natural and usual link of correspondence between the Councils and Conferences with the General Council.

ART. 2. The Upper Council consists of a President, of one or more Vice-Presidents, of a Secretary, a Treasurer, one or several Vice-Secretaries, a Vice-Treasurer, and of several Councillors.

ART. 3. When the President is to be named for the first time, all the Conferences of the circumscription are invited to assist in doing so. The election shall take place under the superintence of the Conference or Council belonging to the town wherein the Upper Council is to be established.

ART. 4. When a new President is to be named,

the Vice-President assembles the Council. This preparatory sitting is devoted to deliberation as to who may be an eligible person for this office. If the former President be still alive, he is invited to designate the person whom he should deem it of advantage to select.

When the members have come to an understanding upon one or several names, the meeting adjourns for a month; during the interval the proceedings of this preparatory meeting are made known to the Presidents of the Particular Councils, who consult their colleagues, and to the Presidents of the Conferences, who consult their respective Councils, or even the Conferences over which they preside; all the Presidents transmit their opinions to the Council, and according to these opinions the Council makes the election; an exact minute of which is recorded. While the election is pending, all the members of the circumscription address, either in private or at the meetings, a special prayer to God, such as the *Veni Creator*, in order that His Spirit may guide them throughout the intended election.

Art. 5. The members of the Upper Council are named, as well as those of the Board, by the President, with the advice of the Council.

Art. 6. The President presides over the Upper

Council, and over the general meetings of the Conferences of the town where it is established. He convenes extraordinary meetings. In case of absence, his place is supplied by the Vice-President, or even, if necessary, by any other member of the Council.

ART. 7. The Secretary keeps an account of the names, Christian names, professions, residences, and dates of reception of the different members of the Conferences belonging to the town where the Upper Council holds its sittings. He also notes down the persons who form the Boards of the Councils, or of the Conferences of the circumscription, as well as the places where, and days and hours when, they hold their sittings.

He draws up the minutes of the sittings held by the Council and general meetings; prepares the annual report upon the works of the Conferences of the circumscription, and transmits it to the General Council. He is entrusted, under the superintendence of the President, with the general correspondence that is kept up with the Presidents and Secretaries of the Councils and Conferences, as well as with the General Council. He has the custody of the records of the Society in that circumscription.

The Treasurer has the care of the funds. He

keeps an exact account of the receipts and expenditure; he submits his accounts to the Council.

ART. 8. In case the Upper Council does not fulfil, for the local Conferences, the office of a Particular Council, the presidency of the latter devolves by right on the President of the Upper Council, who names the Presidents and Vice-Presidents of the Conferences and Special Works, as also the Board of the Particular Council.

In case of any impediment, his presidency over the Particular Council is supplied by a member of the Upper Council, whom he delegates for that purpose.

ART. 9. The funds of the Council are maintained by extraordinary donations made to the Society, by collections at the General Meetings of the town in which it is established, and by the contributions which are annually sent by each Conference, or by each Council of the circumscription, towards the general expenses.

ART. 10. When a Conference or Particular Council is about to be formed in the circumscription, the Upper Council examines how far it may be proper to propose its aggregation to the General Council. This aggregation can never take place but with the previous advice of the Upper Council.

It likewise refers to the General Council, when it is deemed necessary to dissolve any Particular Conference or Council. In a case of urgency, it may temporarily suspend the sittings, and refer the matter to the General Council.

ART. 11. The Upper Council governs all the practical details of the Conferences in the circumscription, either through the medium of correspondence or of circulars from the President, and watches over the observance of the Rules, reserving, however, to the General Council weighty questions, and such as may concern the welfare of the Society at large.

ART. 12. The Presidents of the Upper Councils, when present in Paris, attend at and take part in the sittings of the General Council, of which they are members, as long as they continue to fill the same office.

The General Council may ask for their opinion in writing upon such matters as interest the whole Brotherhood.

PRAYERS.

PRAYERS.

At the Opening of the Meeting.

✠

In the name of the Father, and of the Son, and of the Holy Ghost.   Amen.

Come, O Holy Ghost, fill the hearts of Thy faithful, and enkindle in them the fire of Thy love.

V. Send forth Thy Spirit, and our hearts shall be regenerated.

R. And Thou shalt renew the face of the Earth.

LET US PRAY.

O God, Who, through the light of the Holy Ghost, didst instruct the hearts of the faithful, grant that by the same Spirit we may be truly wise, and ever enjoy His consolation, through Jesus Christ our Lord.   Amen

Ave Maria, etc.

P. St. Vincent de Paul,

R. Pray for us.

In the name, etc.

PRAYERS.

At the Opening of the Meeting.

✠

In nomine Patris, et Filii, et Spiritûs Sancti. Amen.

Veni, Sancte Spiritus:

Reple tuorum corda fidelium, et tui amoris in eis ignem accende.

V. Emitte Spiritum tuum, et creabuntur:

R. Et renovabis faciem terræ.

OREMUS.

Deus, qui corda fidelium Sancti Spiritûs illustratione docuisti, da nobis in eodum Spiritu recta sapere, et de ejus semper consolatione gaudere, per Christum Dominum nostrum.

Ave Maria, etc.

V. Sancte Vincenti à Paulo,

R. Ora pro nobis.

In nomine Patris, etc.

The Closing Prayers.

In the name, etc.
P. St. Vincent de Paul,
R. Pray for us.

LET US PRAY.

Most gracious Jesus, Who didst raise up blessed Vincent for an apostle of Thy most ardent charity in the Church, pour forth upon Thy servants that same fervor of charity, that, for the love of Thee, they may with a most ready heart bestow their goods upon the poor, and spend themselves for their souls: Who with God the Father livest and reignest in the unity of the Holy Ghost, world without end.

R. Amen.

FOR BENEFACTORS.

Vouchsafe, we beseech Thee, Thy grace to the benefactors of the poor, most tender Jesus, Who hast promised a hundredfold and a Heavenly kingdom to those that do works of mercy in Thy name.

R. Amen.

The Closing Prayers.

In nomine Patris, etc.
V. Sancte Vincenti à Paulo,
R. Ora pro nobis.

OREMUS.

Clementissime Jesu qui Beatum Vincentium flagrantissimæ charitatis tuæ apostolum in Ecclesiâ suscitasti, effunde super famulos tuos eumdem charitatis ardorem, ut amore, tuo libentissime in pauperes impendant sua, et seipsos super impendant, qui cum Deo Patre vivis et regnas in unitate Spiritûs Sancti Deus, per omnia sæcula sæculorum. Amen.

PRO BENEFACTORIBUS.

Benefactoribus pauperum gratiam largiri dignare, piissime Jesu, qui impertituris misericordiam in nomine tuo centuplum regnumque cœleste promisisti. Amen.

5*

We fly to thy patronage, O holy Mother
of God : despise not our petitions in our necessities, but deliver us from all dangers, O
ever glorious and blessed Virgin.

R. Amen.

And may the souls of the faithful, through
the mercy of God, rest in peace.

R. Amen.

Queen, conceived without sin, pray for us.

May the Divine assistance remain always
with us.

In the name, etc.

A PRAYER USED BY THE MEMBERS OF THE SOCIETY OF ST. VINCENT DE PAUL.

We thank thee, O Lord! for the graces
and blessings which Thou hast been hitherto
pleased to bestow upon the Society of St.
Vincent de Paul.

We still ask of Thee to grant us these same
blessings for this dear Society, for its several
Conferences, and in particular for the Conference of which we are members. Grant
that our society may be fortified, extended,
and perpetuated, through its primitive spirit

Sub tuum præsidium confugimus, sancta Dei Genitrix : nostras deprecationes ne despicias in necessitatibus ; sed à periculis cunctis libera nos semper, Virgo gloriosa et benedicta. Amen.

Et fidelium animæ per misericordiam Dei requiescant in pace. Amen.

Regina sine labe concepta, ora pra nobis.

In nomine Patris, etc.

A PRAYER USED BY THE MEMBERS OF THE SOCIETY OF ST. VINCENT DE PAUL.*

Gratias agimus tibi, Domine, qui Societatem Sancti Vincentii a Paulo tot ac tantis hactenus benedictionibus cumulare dignatus es.

Hanc igitur nobis dilectissimam Societatem precamur usque respicias, sed et singulas illius partes et eam imprimis cui adscrib-

---

* This prayer was approved of on the 29th of June, 1846, by the Abbè Buquet, Vicar-General of Paris.

of piety, simplicity, and brotherly union, in order that its undertakings, being fully divested of all earthly interest, may become daily more fruitful for Heaven.

Thou knowest, O Lord! the spiritual and temporal misery of the families we endeavor to assist; Thou knowest likewise our own; be pleased to have pity on all, and let all experience the effects of Thy infinite mercy.

We beseech Thee, in particular, O God! to help those amongst our brethren who are undergoing sundry trials; let them never want that strength, that light, that peace and hope which come from Thee; let their trials and our own, which alike proceed from Thee, be supported with patience and resignation, so as to be agreeable to Thy eyes and replete with fruits of salvation.

Lastly, O Lord! we entreat Thee, through the merits of our Lord Jesus Christ, and

imur. Fac, quæsumus, ut propagetur ubique
et in perpetuum confirmetur, vigente semper eodem, qui fuit ab initio, pietatis, sim-
plicitatis et fraternæ dilectionis affectu, ita
ut illius opera, ab omni prorsus terrestri
fœnore et cupiditate libera, magis ac magis
in Cœlum fecundentur.

. Scis ipse, Domine, quam multis indigeant
tum spiritualibus, tum temporalibus, bonis
familiæ pauperum, quibus pro parte, exigua
nimis, opitulamur. Scis et quam multis ipsi
indigeamus. Miserere nostri, Domine, et in-
finitam misericordiam tuam omnes pariter
sentiamus.

Nostris quoque fratribus qui eodum nobis
conjunguntur sodalitio, si qui variis nunc
premuntur angustiis, subveni, piissime Deus.
Infunde illis fortitudinem, prudentiam, pa-
cem et fiduciam quæ a te sunt. Nostræ et
illorum ærumnæ patienter pro Christo tol-
eratæ, tibi sint acceptæ et in salutem fructi-
ficent.

Fusis tandem precibus, te Domine, per
merita Domini nostri Jesu Christi, special-

the special intercession of the Immaculate, Blessed Mary, and of our holy patron, to give one day a place in Thy kingdom to the families of our poor, to our brethren, and to ourselves.   Amen.

emque beatæ Mariæ Immaculatæ et sancti
Vincentii intercessionem deprecamur, ut
solutis nostræ mortalitatis vinculis, omnes
nobis propinquitate seu necessitudine de-
vinctos, pauperes nobis commissos, carissi-
mosque sodales, regni tui nobiscum facias
esse participes. Amen.

THE HYMN, "VENI CREATOR SPIRITUS," AND THE
SEQUENCE, "VENI SANCTE SPIRITUS."

By a Brief dated May 26, 1796, Pope Pius
VI., of blessed memory, granted to all the
faithful who one or more times a day should
invoke the Holy Spirit with the hymn, *Veni
Creator Spiritus*, etc., or the Sequence, *Veni
Sancte Spiritus*, etc., with the intention of
praying for peace amongst Christian princes,

I. THE PLENARY INDULGENCE once a month,
on any one day, after Confession and Communion. Moreover, to those who should recite the said Hymn and Sequence as above
on Whitsunday or during its octave, he
granted—

II. THREE HUNDRED DAYS' INDULGENCE, and

III. ONE HUNDRED DAYS' INDULGENCE daily,
for every other day in the year.

The original Brief above-named is kept
in the Archivium of the Congregation called
Prima Primaria, in the Roman College.

THE HYMN.

Veni Creator Spiritus,
Mentes tuorum visita,
Imple superna gratia,
Quæ Tu creasti pectora.

Qui diceris Paraclitus,
Altissimi Donum Dei,

Fons vivus, Ignis, Charitas,
Et spiritalis Unctio.

Tu septiformis munere,
Digitus Paternæ dexteræ
Tu rite promissum Patris,
Sermone ditans guttura.

Accende lumen sensibus,
Infunde amorem cordibus,
Infirma nostri corporis
Virtute firmans perpeti.

Hostem repellas longius,
Pacemque dones protinus;
Ductore sic Te prævio
Vitemus omne noxium.

Per Te sciamus da Patrem,
Noscamus atque Filium,
Teque utriusque Spiritum
Credamus omni tempore.

Deo Patri sit gloria,
Et Filio, qui a mortuis
Surrexit, ac Paraclito
In sæculorum sæcula.   Amen.

TRANSLATION.

Come, O Creator Spirit!
  Visit this soul of Thine;
This heart of Thy creating
  Fill Thou with grace divine.

Who Paraclete art call'd!
  The gift of God above!
Pure Unction! holy Fire!
  And Fount of life and love,

Finger of God's right hand!
  The Father's promise true!
Who sevenfold gifts bestowest!
  Who dost the tongue endow!

Pour love into our hearts;
  Our senses touch with light;
Make strong our human frailty
  With Thy supernal might.

Cast far our deadly foe;
  Thy peace in us fulfil;
So, Thee before us leading,
  May we escape each ill.

The Father, and the Son,
  Through Thee may we receive;
In Thee, from Both proceeding,
  Through endless time believe.

Praise to the Father be;
  Praise to the Son who rose;
And praise to Thee, blest Spirit!
  While age on ages flows.

THE SEQUENCE.

Veni Sancte Spiritus, et emitte cœlitus lucis
  tuæ radium

Veni Pater pauperum, veni dator munerum,
veni lumen cordium.
Consolator optime, dulcis hospes animæ,
dulce refrigerium.
In labore requies, in æstu temperies, in fletu
solatium.
O lux beatissima, reple cordis intima tuorum fidelium.
Sine tuo numine nihil est in homine, nihil
est innoxium.
Lava quod est sordidum, riga quod est ari-
dum, sana quod est saucium.
Flecte quod est rigidum, fove quod est fri-
gidum, rege quod est devium.
Da tuis fidelibus in te confidentibus sacrum
septenarium.
Da virtutis meritum, da salutis exitum, da
perenne gaudium.   Amen.

TRANSLATION.

Holy Spirit! Lord of light!
From Thy clear celestial height,
   Thy pure beaming radiance give:

Come, Thou Father of the poor!
Come, with treasures which endure!
   Come, Thou Light of all that live!

Thou, of all consolers best,
Visiting the troubled breast,
   Dost refreshing peace bestow;

Thou in toil art comfort sweet;
Pleasant coolness in the heat;
  Solace in the midst of woe.

Light immortal! Light Divine!
Visit Thou these hearts of Thine,
  And our inmost being fill:

If Thou take Thy grace away,
Nothing pure in man will stay;
  All his good is turn'd to ill.

Heal our wounds—our strength renew;
On our dryness pour thy dew;
  Wash the stains of guilt away:

Bend the stubborn heart and will;
Melt the frozen, warm the chill;
  Guide the steps that go astray.

Thou, on those who evermore
Thee confess and Thee adore,
  In Thy sevenfold gifts, descend:

Give them comfort when they die;
Give them life with Thee on high;
  Give them joys which never end.

THE "DE PROFUNDIS" AT THE FIRST HOUR AFTER NIGHTFALL.

Pope Clement XII. was the first who, in order to move the piety of Christians to pray for the souls in Purgatory, granted, by a Brief of Aug. 14, 1736, *Cœlestes Ecclesiœ thesauros—*

I. The Indulgence of 100 days to all the faithful, every time that at the sound of the bell, at the first hour after nightfall, they say devoutly on their knees the psalm *De Profundis*, with a *Requiem æternam* at the end of it.

II. The Plenary Indulgence to those who perform this pious exercise at the hour appointed for a whole year, once in the year, on any one day, after having Confessed and Communicated. Those who do not know by heart the *De Profundis*, may gain these Indulgences by saying in the way already mentioned for the *De Profundis* one *Pater Noster* and one *Ave Maria*, with the *Requiem æternam*.

Observe also, that the aforesaid Clement XII. declared, Dec. 12, 1736, that these Indulgences might be gained by saying the *De Profundis*, etc., as above, although, according to the custom of a particular church or place, the "signal for the dead," as it is called, be given by the sound of the bell either before or after one hour after nightfall.

Pope Pius VI., by a Rescript of March 18, 1781, granted the above-named Indulgences to all the faithful who should chance

6*

to dwell in any place where no bell for the dead is sounded, and shall yet say the *De Profundis* or *Pater Noster*, etc., as aforesaid, about nightfall.

Psalm cxxix.

De profundis clamavi ad te, Domine : *
Domine, exaudi vocem meam.

Fiant aures tuæ intendentes * in vocem deprecationis meæ.

Si iniquitates observaveris, Domine : * Domine, quis sustinebit?

Quia apud te propitiatio est : * et propter legem tuam sustinui te, Domine.

Sustinuit anima mea in verbo ejus : * speravit anima mea in Domino.

A custodia matutina usque ad noctem * speret Israel in Domino.

Quia apud Dominum misericordia, * et copiosa apud eum redemptio.

Et ipse redimet Israel * ex omnibus iniquitatibus ejus.

Requiem æternam * dona eis, Domine.

Et lux perpetua luceat eis.

Requiescant in pace.

Amen.

End at pleasure with the following.

V. Domine, exaudi orationem meam,
R. Et clamor meus ad te veniat.

Oremus.

Fidelium Deus omnium conditor et re-
demptor, animabus famulorum famularum-
que tuarum remissionem cunctorum tribue
peccatorum : ut indulgentiam, quam semper optaverunt, piis supplicationibus conse
quantur. Qui vivis et regnas in sæcula sæculorum.

R. Amen.

V. Requiem æternam dona eis, Domine.

R. Et lux perpetua luceat eis.

V. Requiescant in pace.

R. Amen.

Psalm cxxix.

Out of the depths I have cried to Thee, O
Lord : Lord, hear my voice.

Let Thine ears hearken : to the voice of
my supplication.

If Thou, O Lord, shalt mark our iniquities : O Lord, who can abide it?

For with Thee there is mercy : and by
reason of Thy law I have waited on Thee,
O Lord.

My soul hath waited on His word : my
soul hath hoped in the Lord.

From the morning watch even unto night:
let Israel hope in the Lord.

For with the Lord there is mercy: and with Him plenteous redemption.

And He shall redeem Israel: from all his iniquities.

Eternal rest give to them, O Lord.

And let perpetual light shine upon them.

May they rest in peace.

Amen.

V. Lord hear my prayer,

R. And let my cry come unto Thee.

Let us pray.

O God, the Creator and Redeemer of all the faithful; grant to the souls of Thy servants and Thy handmaids departed the remission of all their sins, that through the devout prayers of Thy Church on earth they may obtain that remission of pain which they have ever desired. Who livest and reignest world without end. Amen.

V. Eternal rest give to them, O Lord.

R. And let everlasting light enlighten them.

V. May they rest in peace.

R. Amen.

Five Pater *and* Ave, *with the* V. Te ergo, *etc.*

INDULGENCES

GRANTED TO

The Society of St. Vincent de Paul,

AND TO

THE BENEFACTORS OF THIS SOCIETY, BY THE BRIEFS
OF THE SOVEREIGN PONTIFFS GREGORY
XVI. AND PIUS IX., DATED
January 10, *August* 12, 1845 ; *March* 18, 1853 ; *and*
March 28, 1854.

SECTION FIRST.—INDULGENCES GRANTED TO THE MEMBERS OF THE SOCIETY.

A PLENARY INDULGENCE once each month to the Members of the General Council, and of the Particuler Council of Paris and of any other city, who, besides complying with the usual conditions, shall have been present at all, or three out of the four meetings of their Council held during the month.

A PLENARY INDULGENCE once each month to all active members, on the usual conditions, and provided they shall have been present at all, or at three out of the four Conference Meetings held during the month. This indulgence can also be gained by the Members of Councils who may already have gained the above-mentioned indulgence.

A PLENARY INDULGENCE on the day of reception as an Aspirant Member, an Ordinary Member, or Member of any particular Council, or of the General Council, the usual conditions having been complied with.

A Plenary Indulgence to both active and honorary Members, who, on the festival of the Immaculate Conception of the Blessed Virgin Mary, or, if it is transferred, on the day itself on which it is celebrated; and of St. Vincent of Paul, and the seven days immediately following, once only during this space of eight days, and on the second Sunday after Easter, and on the Monday after the first Sunday in Lent, being truly penitent and having confessed their sins, shall receive the Holy Sacrament at the Mass which, on the aforesaid days, is celebrated for the Society, and shall have been present at the General Meeting which is held on those occasions.

A Plenary Indulgence at the hour of death to all members of this Society, who, being truly penitent, and confessing their sins, or, should circumstances prevent their doing this, being at least contrite, shall with their lips, or, if unable to do so, in their hearts, devoutly invoke the *holy Name of Jesus*, and shall, with a patient and ready mind, accept death from the hand of the Lord as a penalty for sin.

An Indulgence of Seven Years and as many Forty Days, as often as an active member shall, with at least a contrite heart, visit any conference or poor family, or the schools or work shops of the poor, or perform any other good work in accordance with the spirit of the Society, or shall assist at the holy sacrifice of the Mass, when celebrated for the soul of any member, or shall follow the bodies of the poor to ecclesiastical interment.

The above Indulgences extend to members who live in places where as yet no Conference exists, provided they perform, as far as they can, the customary works, and fulfil the other prescribed conditions.

A PLENARY INDULGENCE to all members who have attended devoutly each day to the spiritual exercises which take place for the members collectively, and who, being truly penitent, and having confessed, shall receive the Holy Communion at the Mass on the last of these days, and offer prayers for the concord of Christian princes, the uprooting of heresies, and the exaltation of our Holy Mother the Church.

AN INDULGENCE OF ONE HUNDRED DAYS to the members who, contrite in heart, shall have fulfilled only a part of the spiritual exercises, and shall have prayed as above.

N. B. All the above Indulgences may be applied by way of suffrage to the souls in Purgatory.

SECTION SECOND.—INDULGENCES GRANTED TO THE BENEFACTORS OF THE SOCIETY.

1°. A PLENARY INDULGENCE once a month to all and every one of the faithful, whether men or women, who shall regularly give to the General Council some fixed alms, provided they be truly penitent, confess their sins, and receive the Holy Communion.

2°. AN INDULGENCE OF SEVEN YEARS AND AS MANY FORTY DAYS, once each month, to all the faithful, whether men or women, who shall regularly transmit some fixed alms, to the Particular

Councils of Provinces or Towns established by the General Council.

3°. AN INDULGENCE OF ONE YEAR, obtainable, likewise, once each month by such of the faithful, men or women, who shall, in writing or otherwise, engage to give regularly some fixed alms to Conferences approved by the General Council, or by Particular Councils empowered to approve by the General Council.

4°. AN INDULGENCE OF SEVEN YEARS AND AS MANY FORTY DAYS, to all the faithful, whether men or women, obtainable once each month, on the days when they solicit and collect contributions in aid of the Councils, whether General or Particular.

5°. A PLENARY INDULGENCE at the hour of death to all benefactors of the Society, who, being truly penitent, and confessing their sins, or, should circumstances prevent their doing this, being at least contrite, shall, with their lips, or, if unable so to do, in their hearts, devoutly invoke *the Holy Name of Jesus*, and shall with a patient and ready mind accept death from the hand of the Lord as a penalty for sin.

Declared to be in conformity with the Apostolic Letters: *Romanum decet Pontificem* of January 10th, 1845; *Cum Societatem* of August 12th, of the same year; *Exponendum nobis curarunt sodales* of March 18th, 1853; and *Exponendum nobis curarunt dilecti filii* of March 28th, 1854.   (Signed)   L. BUQUET,

PARIS, February 12th, 1855.   *Vicar-General.*

Society of St. Vincent de Paul

EXPLANATORY NOTES

THE ARTICLES

OF

THE GENERAL RULE

OF

THE SOCIETY.

(From the French.)

PRINTED FOR THE COUNCIL OF NEW YORK,
BY EDWARD DUNIGAN & BROTHER
(JAMES B. KIRKER,)
599 BROADWAY, N. YORK.
1869.

THE BRIEF

Of His Holiness Pope Gregory XVI., to the Council-General of the Society of St. Vincent de Paul.

GREGORY XVI., POPE.

For the perpetual remembrance of the thing.

It becometh the Roman Pontiff to enrich, in a special manner, with the heavenly treasures of the Church, those pious societies that labor with all care and zeal in the performance of works of Christian charity. Wherefore, having been earnestly solicited by the President and Council-General of the Society of St. Vincent de Paul, which was originally established in Paris, to grant to that Society some indulgences, as well plenary as partial. We have thought fit that their pious supplication should be freely acceded to.

Wherefore we mercifully grant, in the Lord, a plenary indulgence to all and every the members, whether attached to the now instituted Council-General at Paris, of the said Society, or to particular Councils of Paris and other cities, who, being truly penitent, shall have confessed their sins and received the Holy Communion; provided that they shall have been present at all, or at three out of the four meetings of the Council which are holden in the month.

Further, to all active members, as they are termed, of the Society itself, and also the members of the Councils, and others of whom mention has been above made, who may have previously obtained the aforesaid indulgence. We in like manner grant a plenary indulgence, provided that they shall have been present at all, or at three out of the four meetings or conferences holden in the month, and that being truly penitent, and having confessed their sins, they shall have received the most Holy Sacrament of the Eucharist. Moreover, we likewise grant the same plenary indulgence, to be gained by all persons to be admitted into the aforesaid Society on that day, on which, being in like manner truly penitent, and having confessed their sins, and having received the Holy Communion, they shall have been received into the different active grades of aspirant member, ordinary member, member of a Particular Council, or of the Council-General. Moreover, we likewise grant a plenary indulgence to all members, as well active as honorary, of the said Society, who, on the Feast of the Im-

maculate Conception of the Blessed Virgin Mary, and of St.
Vincent de Paul, and on the second Sunday after Easter,
which is the anniversary of the translation of the relics of the
same St. Vincent ; as also on the Monday after the first Sunday of Lent, being truly penitent, and having confessed their
sins, shall have received the Holy Communion, at the Mass
which is celebrated on these aforesaid days for the Society,
and shall have been present at the general meeting which is
holden at these seasons.   And also in like manner, we grant
a plenary·indulgence to all the members and benefactors of
the Society, who, at the hour of death, being truly penitent,
and having confessed their sins, or if unable to do so, being
at least contrite, shall have devoutly invoked the name of
Jesus with their lips, if able, but if not, with their heart, and
with a patient and ready spirit shall have received death from
the hand of the Lord as the wages of sin.   Moreover, we remit, according to the usual form of the Church, seven years,
and as many quarantines of the penances enjoined on them,
or otherwise in any way due by them, to all active members
of the same Society, as often, as at least with a contrite heart,
they shall have visited any conference, any poor family, or
the schools and workshops of the poor, or shall have performed any other good work, according to the spirit of the
said Society ; which partial indulgence the active members of
the aforesaid Society can each gain, as often as with a contrite
heart they shall attend at the Holy Sacrifice of the Mass,
offered up for the soul of any member. and as often as they
shall have accompanied the bodies of poor persons to ecclesiastical sepulture.   All and singular these indulgences and
relaxations of penances, we allow to be applicable by way of
suffrage to the souls of the faithful of Christ, who shall have
departed life united in charity with God.   Finally, by the
same, our Apostolic authority, we give and grant all and
each of the aforesaid indulgences to all other Councils and
Conferences of the same Society which, with the approbation
of the Council-General, are instituted, whether by the Council-General itself or by the Particular Councils of cities or of
provinces already instituted by the Council-General ; also to
members who live in places wherein a Conference is not yet
established, if in such places they shall have performed as far
as they are able, the usual works, and shall have complied
with the other conditions already prescribed.   Our rule, and
the rule of the Apostolical Chancery, of not granting indulgences *ad instar*, and the other Apostolical constitutions and
ordinances, and all other things to the contrary hereof, not·
withstanding.   And we also wish that transcripts or copies,
even printed ones, of these letters, bearing the signature of

a person of ecclesiastical dignity, may moreover receive the same credit as would be given to these letters, were they produced and shown.

Given at Rome, at St. Peter's, under the Fisherman's Ring, the 10th day of January, 1845, in the fourteenth year of our Pontificate.

(Place of ✠ the Seal.)

A. CARD. LAMBRUSCHINI.

Approved as a faithful translation of the Brief of his Holiness Gregory XVI.—Brooklyn, January 1, 1855.

✠ JOHN, Bishop of Brooklyn.

(*Seal.*)

Further Brief of His Holiness Pope Gregory XVI., to the Council-General of the Society of St. Vincent de Paul.

GREGORY XVI., POPE.

For the perpetual remembrance of the thing.

Whereas, the Society instituted under the auspices and name of St. Vincent de Paul, and devoted to the performance of works of Christian charity, to our knowledge conduces in an eminent degree to the good of religion and the advantage of the faithful, we, in order that it may from day to day receive fresh increase, have thought fit, that out of the celestial treasures of the Church, all those should be enriched who shall have contributed their exertions and means in aid of this Society, so that this their zeal may become more and more ardent by the holding forth of spiritual favors. Wherefore, we mercifully grant, in the Lord, a plenary indulgence, once in the month, to all and singular the faithful of Christ of either sex, who, being truly penitent, and having confessed their sins, and received the Holy Communion, transmit a fixed and constant eleemosynary donation to the Council-General. Moreover, we grant an indulgence of seven years and of as many quarantines once in the month, to all Christ's faithful of either sex, who shall transmit a fixed and constant eleemosynary donation of this kind to the Particular Councils of provinces or cities instituted by the Council-General. Moreover, we grant an indulgence of one year to be gained likewise, once in the month, to Christ's faithful of either sex,

who by writing, or in any other way, engage to contribute
any fixed and constant eleemosynary donation to Conferences
approved of either by the Council-General or by the Particular
Councils delegated for this purpose.   Finally, we grant an indulgence of seven years and of as many quarantines, to all
and singular the faithful of Christ of either sex, to be gained
once in the month on those days, to wit, on which they shall
have collected by questing, a pecuniary alms for the Council-
General or Particular Councils.   Our rule, and the rule of the
Apostolical Chancery, of not granting indulgences *ad instar*,
and the other Apostolical constitutions and ordinances, and
all other things to the contrary hereof, notwithstanding.
And we also wish that transcripts or copies, even printed ones,
of these letters, bearing the signature of a person of ecclesiastical dignity, may moreover receive the same credit as would
be given to these letters, were they produced and shown.

Given at Rome, at St. Mary Major's, under the Fisherman's
Ring, the 12th August, 1845, in the fifteenth year of our Pontificate.

(Place of ✠ the Seal.)

A. CARD. LAMBRUSCHINI, *Bishop of Sabine.*

Approved as a faithful translation of the Brief of His Holiness Gregory XVI.—Brooklyn, January 1st, 1855.

✠ JOHN. Bishop of Brooklyn.

(*Seal.*)

BRIEF

Of Our Holy Father, Pope Pius the Ninth,

Granting an extension of Indulgence to the Society of St. Vincent de Paul.

And attaching new indulgences to the recitation of certain prayers, whether by the members of the Society, or by the families they visit.

PIUS THE NINTH, POPE,

For the perpetual remembrance of the thing.

THE Council General (holding its sittings in Paris) of the charitable Society, which bears the name of St. Vincent de Paul, has represented to us, that by Apostolic letters of the date of January, 1845, a plenary indulgence was accorded to all and every one of the faithful (being members of the said Society), to be gained (under the usual conditions) once in every year, on the Feast of the Immaculate Conception of the Virgin Mary, Mother of God, and on the Monday succeeding the first Sunday in Lent.

By those same letters it was further granted, that the faithful above-mentioned might equally gain a plenary indulgence, if on the stated festivals of the Society, after having performed according to rule the other required works of charity, they are present at the Mass then celebrated for the said Society.

But the Council aforesaid having brought to our notice that it would be of advantage to the members, if the two

(vii)

plenary indulgences above-mentioned, should be transferred
to another day, and that the condition required to obtain
the second of the said indulgences, namely, the attendance
at Mass, should be modified to a certain extent, and We
having been entreated to concede, by virtue of our Apostolical Authority, as well to the said Society as to the
faithful entrusted to its care, new helps to their eternal
salvation; We who have singularly at heart all pious associations which while they relieve the immediate necessities
of the poor, prepare and form their souls to virtue, have
thought proper to assent to these and similar requests.
Wherefore, confiding in the mercy of Almighty God, and
relying upon the authority of the Holy Apostles, Peter
and Paul, We extend the plenary indulgence which the
said associates can gain on the day of the Feast of the
Immaculate Conception of the Blessed Virgin Mary, to
the Sunday immediately following, provided this Feast
does not fall on a Sunday, or is not, in the locality, transferred to some other Sunday—in such manner that the
said members may at their option gain the plenary indulgence either on the day of the Immaculate Conception, or
the Sunday next thereafter succeeding.

We also, by virtue of these presents, transfer the plenary
indulgence granted for the first Monday in Lent to the
Sunday immediately preceding, supposing the other conditions to be maintained entire.

And further, lest in any place the scarcity of priests
should present an obstacle, We concede by this Brief
that the said members, though the Mass which they
hear shall not have been celebrated at the instance of the
said Society, shall, if they have duly complied with the
other condition, equally acquire a plenary indulgence in
the Lord.

Furthermore, in virtue of the fullness of the same Apostolic Power, we mercifully grant in the Lord a plenary

indulgence and remission of all their sins to all and every one of the faithful of both sexes, to whom the said Society may extend its aid, who being truly penitent and having confessed, shall have received Holy Communion, and shall have visited devoutly any Church or public Oratory, on the day of the Feast of the Nativity of our Blessed Lord, or on the day of the Feast of St. Joseph, the Spouse of the Blessed Virgin Mary from the hour of early vespers; and on the day of the close of the annual exercises denominated the Spiritual Retreat, from the rising to the setting of the Sun; offering up to God on these occasions fervent prayers for the concord of Christian princes, the extirpation of heresies, and the exaltation of our Holy Mother, the Church.

Finally, we remit, in the customary form to all and every one of the faithful, connected, under any title, with this benevolent Society, and also to its benefactors three hundred days of penances enjoined or in any way incurred, as often as, having at least a contrite heart, they recite in any language the prayer peculiar to the Society, which begins thus: "*Gratias agimus*," "We thank thee, O Lord, for the graces and blessings which Thou hast been hitherto pleased to bestow upon the Society of St. Vincent de Paul." And to all persons assisted by the said Society, we remit one hundred days of penance enjoined or in any way incurred, provided that having at least a contrite heart, they recite, either alone, or with their families, one *Our Father*, and one *Hail Mary*, with the addition (in any language) of the following invocations:

"Queen conceived without the stain of original sin, pray for us!" "St. Vincent de Paul, pray for us!"

And we allow, moreover, all these indulgences, remissions of sin, and relaxations of penance, to be applied by way of suffrage to the souls of the faithful departed in the grace of God.

And these presents shall remain binding now and in all future time, anything that may be said or done in opposition to them to the contrary notwithstanding.

It is also our will that copies, whether manuscript or printed, of these presents, signed by a Notary public, and attested by the seal of a person constituted of ecclesiastical dignity, shall obtain the same credit and have the same effect that the original would have if produced and exhibited.

Given at Rome, at St. Peters, under the Fisherman's Ring, the 13th day of September, 1859, in the fourteenth year of our Pontificate.

For His Eminence CARDINAL MACCHI.

Jo. B. BRANCALEONI,

CASTELLANI, *Subst.*

☞ The above is stamped with the seal of the Apostolic *Nunciature* and certified as follows:

" It agrees with the original.

PARIS, June 5th, 1861.

F. XAV. COMPIETA,

Sec. Apost. Nunciat.

The above is a correct translation of the original.

WM. STARRS, *Adm'r.*

NEW YORK, *March* 3, 1864.

INTRODUCTION.

THE spirit of an association is to be found particularly in its rule, and if it extend, and be perpetuated, it becomes necessary to fix its usages by positive regulations, and not to leave the observance of them to depend any longer upon the interpretation of individuals, necessarily variable as it would be. This it was which, eighteen years ago, made the early members of the Society of St. Vincent de Paul draw up the Rule which, saving such modifications in the details as time has necessarily brought into it, governs it up to the present day.

But in order that a rule should last, it is not of less consequence to know its precise purposes than its general tendencies; for, if the letter should never destroy the spirit, nevertheless the former is an element necessary to the understanding of the primitive and fundamental idea.

But, for a long time past, complaints have been made in the Society of St. Vincent de Paul, that the Rule *itself* is not understood; that its *articles*, although placed under every eye, *are not known;* and consequently that old traditions are very often departed from unintentionally. As this evil actually exists, it has been considered that it would be easily remedied by publishing some explanatory notes upon the different articles of the General Rule. By collecting under each article the passages of the Circulars

1*

which refer to it, the usages made sacred by tradition, the additions made by force of circumstances, it is hoped that a new interest will be given to the reading of these articles, naturally somewhat dry as they are, and that consequently they will be resorted to more frequently in the Conferences and by the members themselves.

This is the sole motive of the following pages. The intention in getting them up was not by any means to devote one's self to a minute and subtle study of texts, but to bring out plainly the spirit of the Society, which, without doubt, is still more strongly expressed in the general considerations prefixed to the Rule, and which is also visible in each of the articles. The perusal of this will probably be more and more convincing that this spirit is one of entire simplicity, cordiality, self-denial, and in this sense it will certainly be useful. That it may fructify more, it is dedicated to the Immaculate Patroness of our Society the ever-blessed Virgin Mary, one of whose principal festivals the Church celebrates to-day.

21st November, 1853,
Feast of the Presentation of
The Blessed Virgin.

EXPLANATORY NOTES

THE GENERAL RULE.

--------◆--------

ARTICLE 1.—All Christian young men who desire to unite in a communion of prayers and a participation of the same works of charity, may become members of the Society of Saint Vincent de Paul, wherever they may happen to reside.

This article, the object of which is to set forth the aim and the nature of the Society, contains many points of the highest importance.

Firstly, it recalls to mind that the Society of St. Vincent de Paul has been founded by *young men and for them;* it is with a view of preserving them from the dangers of every kind that surround them at the commencement of their career, that Conferences have been organized; and if, at a later time, men of more advanced age have come to join themselves to them, and to bring to them the tribute of their experience, we should not be the less mindful of the original aim of the Society, and we should seek, as much as possible, to attract to it young men, those especially who, far from their own families, have need of being surrounded by a pious circle to make them persevere in good.—(*Circular of 1st November*, 1851, *page* 362.)

It results, moreover, from this article, that the Conferences are intended for men only; that women cannot take part in them, either as active or as honorary members. By a natural consequence, the works of women, although founded upon a rule analogous to that of the men, cannot be aggregated to the Society. Conferences may have charitable relations with them, may adopt the cases of the poor whom they recommend, and may recommend others to them in turn; but they must keep separate their government, their resources, their meetings. It will be seen further on, that women can become benefactresses to the Society, and in that relation participate in numerous Indulgences.

The article adds that the members must be *Christians*, and the 18th article confirms it by adding, that " each member should be careful not to introduce into the Society any one who will not edify his fellow-members or be edified by them. All should strive to love each other, and the poor like brothers." The Council-General, interpreting the rule, has always understood that this condition could not be considered as fulfilled but among men, Christians not only in feeling but in practice, fulfilling all the duties prescribed by the Church, and especially the Paschal duty. On this subject almost all the *Circulars* may be consulted, in particular those of the 14*th July*, 1841, and of the 31*st May*, 1846. Good sense, moreover, proves it in an evident manner. One of the aims of the Society being to make the poor better men and better Christians, how can one effect this if he is not so himself, and how can he inculcate duties which he does not discharge?

It is, moreover, to be remarked, that the primary object which the Society proposes to its members, is their own edification. If they meet together, if they visit the poor, the first object is to make each other better *by an union in prayer*. The aim of the Conferences is not, then, philanthropy, the alleviation—very praiseworthy, no doubt, but purely human—of the sufferings of the poor ; their aim is zeal for the salvation of souls, and in particular for the souls of the members themselves. This is a point which must never be lost sight of, for numerous consequences spring from it, especially in the selection of the works to be undertaken by Conferences, which ought all to tend towards the sanctification of the members engaged in them.

Still, if charitable works are not the primary object of the Society, they are the principal means made use of to attain that object. There are some associations which are conducive to the sanctification of those engaged in them, as pious congregations, by their frequent and prolonged prayers; there are others that strive to the same end by charitable exercises and by penance united to prayer, such as the Third Orders. The Society of St. Vincent de Paul has not so high an aim; it does not aspire to be a congregation, a confraternity, a Third Order; it is no more than a pious assembly of Christians living in the world, and desiring to put their purity under the shelter of charity. To ask more for it would be to pervert its character and its institution.

The Council-General has been consulted several times to know if it were expedient to admit as members persons who were not above want. It has always replied in the negative (*see the Circular of the* 14*th July*, 1841). Doubtless it is not necessary to be favored by fortune in order to take part in the Society. With regard to this, much consideration must be given to the locality in which the particular conference accomplishes its works. For example: the conditions could not be absolutely the same in a poor country district as in a large city; but it is always of consequence that the member should be in a position to help the poor in some degree, however small, and should never have need to be himself assisted. Every one can comprehend the inconvenience which may arise from a contrary usage.

The last words of the article which occupies our attention, "in whatsoever country found," add a new feature most essential to the Society—that is, its universality. Intimately united to the Church, its ambition is to serve it, everywhere and forever, without distinction of race or of country, without difference of language or of government. If there be any thing which can unite men by a bond, at once the strongest and the purest, surely it is charity, that eternal charm of angels and of men, as St. Vincent de Paul called it.

2.—No work of charity should be regarded as foreign to the Society, although its special object is to visit poor families. Thus, its members are expected to embrace every opportunity of affording consolation to the sick and to prisoners, of instructing poor, unprotected, or imprisoned children, and of procuring the succors of religion for those who need them, at the hour of .death.

In this is presented an application of the principle already referred to—namely, that the Society, above all things, aims at the sanctification of its members. If, in fact, visiting poor families is its most special, indeed, its fundamental work, it is because that is the work which is the most conducive to the edification of the members, and that which is most within their reach. Undoubtedly, it is very meritorious to undertake the patronage of children, or to facilitate marriages among the poor, but the exercise of these works has not the same practical effect *upon the members* as visiting the poor in their garrets, their cellars, or their cabins. To undertake these works, it is necessary, in some sort, to have carried out the visiting of the poor; otherwise, insurmountable difficulties would arise in them, were it but those of inexperience alone, and members would get a distaste for these works, whether on account of being frustrated in them, or because too much time was absorbed in them. On the other hand, visiting the poor attaches one to it, captivates one, because it always produces immediate results, material relief; it is easily practised, and requires but little time. For all these reasons, it ought to be the favorite work of a society composed of men who live in the world, and are engaged in numerous occupations; and this is why the Circulars constantly recommend it.

It is well to remark, also, that if no work of charity should be regarded as foreign to the Society, this expression is always to be understood with this reservation, *that the work should be suited to the special character of the Society.* Thus it has constantly been regarded as an imperative rule, not to undertake any work relating to females, particularly such as are young and live alone. The Society leaves the care of them, as well as the patronage of schools for young girls, to ladies' associations, or to the indefatigable zeal of the clergy. Moreover, when commencing new works, the rules of prudence should never be forgotten. It is most desirable that every Conference should exert itself to add some new work to those already in operation; but in doing so, the step should be taken without precipitation, and when the necessary means exist. Our rule should be, neither tepidity nor rashness.

3.—When several members of the Society are found in any locality, they meet to encourage each other in the practice of virtue. This meeting 'is called a *Conference*, the name originally given to the Society itself.

The Circular of the 1st December, 1842, referring to the origin of the title given to our meetings, of *Conferences*, which is that usually given at Paris to literary assemblies of young people, insists very earnestly that the Society should occupy itself exclusively with *practising* charity, instead of discussing systems for the relief of the poor. It will be useful to repeat here that passage which puts forward one of the essential points of our organization: "It is not our office to instruct each other by discourses, but it is to give examples for mutual edification. Do not allow the spirit of discussion, the habits of the tribune, to get among us. We do not mean to find fault with this spirit in itself; discussion is good and necessary, when used in places and applied to subjects which need it, but our Society is a working society; it should do much, and speak little. Let us leave to our officers, to our councils, the troublesome task of discussing whatever is susceptible of debate; let our Conferences, in a body, keep for themselves the consoling charge of good works."

Every Conference which desires to obtain admission into the Society must solicit aggregation from the Council-General, adding to its request a list of its members, an account of its first works, as well as the date of its formation, and an expression of its intention to conform to the regulations and usages of the Society. This request is forwarded directly, if the Conference be in a town where there is neither a Particular, a Central, nor an Upper

Council; otherwise it is forwarded by the proper Council, who add a favorable or unfavorable opinion upon it.

If the aggregation be advisable, the Council-General declares it. By the simple fact of this aggregation the new Conference participates in the Indulgences granted by the Holy See. Without the completion of this indispensable formality, it would be deprived of them.

Moreover, nothing is more useful than this organization. If there were not unity in the aggregations, the Society would be very quickly liable to become a mere agglomeration of several associations, having no spirit in common, possessing an identity in name only, and in which the most experienced eye could not detect the signs of relationship. The recommendations of the different local Councils, when they exist, is also a useful precaution, since it guarantees to the Council-General the good internal organization of the new Conferences, which could only be known upon the spot.

4.—Should several Conferences be formed in the same town, each takes the name of the parish where its members meet, and the several Conferences are united by a *Particular Council*, which takes the name of the town itself.

The principle laid down by Article 4, of the parochial denomination given to the Conferences, is a result of the essentially Catholic character of the Society. As an obedient child of the Church, it connects itself as much as is possible to her imperishable hierarchy.

5.—All the Conferences of the Society are united by a Council-General.

This is the place to explain shortly the organization of the Society.

Its foundations are the Conferences, which are occupied in practical works.

Over the Conferences, where there are several in the same town, is a Particular Council, the constitution of which will appear further on.

Over the Particular Council (as well as over isolated

ferences) is either a Central Council or an Upper Council, embracing within its circumscription the Conferences of several dioceses or of an entire country.

In fine, a Council-General, the centre of the whole Society, being a bond of union, a means of unity, and devoting the time and zeal of its members to the common interest.

In this way, each Conference is not isolated, and is not left to itself alone. It has not to form its rule, its traditions, without taking advice of any one; on the contrary, it forms part of a great Society, between the members of which there exists unity of heart, of intention, of customs; it rests upon the experience of other Conferences, upon the enlightened decisions of the different Councils; and while, in carrying out its own works, it preserves the fullest liberty of action, it enjoys the benefits of a direction common to and accepted by all.

Need it be added, that the authority of the different Councils, from the Particular Council up to the Council-General, is an actual authority, only because it is spontaneously accepted, and that persuasion and good example are the surest, not to say the sole means of supporting their authority. The Church, nevertheless, has wished to give strength to these ties in the manner which is the most effectual for Christians, by granting most valuable Indulgences to Conferences and Councils instituted by the Council-General. This is the object of the two Briefs of the 10th January and 12th August, 1845.

2

CHAPTER I.

THE CONFERENCES.

6.—The Conferences meet upon such days and at such hours as they themselves may appoint.

The fullest latitude is allowed in this matter to the Conferences themselves, for nothing is more variable than the convenience of different localities, and it is of great importance that choice should be made of a day which is the most convenient to the greatest number; otherwise the meetings would run the risk of being little frequented, and consequently zeal and charity would relax.

This is, however, the occasion to be precise upon a point to which the Council-General attaches much importance—that is, the weekly periodical occurrence of the meetings. As the rules do not lay down this period expressly, an inference has been sometimes drawn, that meetings need only take place every fortnight or every month. Except rural Conferences, where, on account of the distance, the difficulty of the roads, or different local circumstances, meetings every eight days would be at times too troublesome, the Council-General has not ceased to exhort Conferences to meet every eight days, as has been the rule since the commencement of the Society, and as it is almost the universal practice. The object of our meetings is, as has been already said, to form, above all things, Christian relations among the members, and to strengthen them in piety by mutual good example. But a meeting every fortnight, and still more, every month, is inadequate to such a result, when, moreover, deductions must be made for the absences, more or less numerous, to which sickness, business, or travelling, cannot fail to compel members. The result would be, that at the end of a year they would scarcely have seen, scarcely have known each other; and many years may go on in this way without that Christian intimacy which the Society has in view, being formed among the members. Thus the Conferences in which the meetings are far apart, are more cold and more languishing. In the others, on the contrary, a greater affection becomes felt towards the brothers, and the work which is in common among them, because they meet together for it oftener; and they assist in it with greater assiduity, because that assiduity becomes more habitual, and because they feel greater satisfaction in it. Moreover, the interests of the poor are better cared for when meetings which are to be occupied with them take place every eight days, and the treasury of the Conference is better furnished, because the collection, made oftener, becomes of necessity more abundant. The strongest reasons concur, then, in favor of meeting weekly, and it is desirable that for towns it should be the rule without any exception. But even when a departure from this custom is necessary, as in certain rural districts, it is important to remark that the visit to the poor should always be weekly. Without a visit made at least once a week, it would be almost impossible to have a constant knowledge of the wants of the poor, and to acquire over them an influence which would be salutary for the amelioration of their habits.

7.—The Conferences should endeavor to carry on a correspondence with each other for their mutual edification and support, and that they may be able, whenever necessary, to recommend to the kind offices of each other, either the members themselves of the Society, or other young men, or the poor families who change their places of abode.

The habit of frequent communication between one Conference and another is one of those which has contributed most to the development of the Society, and which should be most sedulously kept up. Relations will be perhaps less intimate as the Society progresses than at the time when it was exchanged between seven or eight

Conferences, formed by persons all of whom were mutually acquainted; but it ought not to have less cordiality and freedom, since, as has been said, the Society of St. Vincent de Paul is a ready-made friendship, and in entering into it, one, as it were, comes among a closely united family circle. It is, moreover, to facilitate these familiar intercommunications, that the Society has been subdivided as has been shown already. The Conferences, being formed into groups under Central Councils and Upper Councils, should consider that it is by no means intended to segregate each from the common and the sole centre, the Council-General, but to bring them together one to another; for, among twelve hundred Conferences spread over all the world, intimate relations are not possible in reality, and they can only have very rare occasions of communication; but between twenty or thirty Conferences near each other, these communications should be as frequent as they are easy.

The object of this correspondence is, before every thing, to give mutual edification, to communicate to each other the good which each witnesses; thus the blessed innovations of zeal do not remain isolated, but become propagated, and thereby works become general and are extended. This is then a cardinal point in the Society of St. Vincent de Paul, since that which is most wanted in what is good, is not that it should be practised by this one or that, but that it should be known to all, in order that it may be put into application by all those who desire to do so. These intercommunications take place by means of the visits of members, by printed reports, or still further, through the Circulars, the General Report, and the Monthly Bulletin of the Society. Of course, all these communications ought to be simple, modest, and should never become, either for the members or for the Society, a subject from which may be drawn any vain glory for the little good done. St. Vincent de Paul desired that his missionaries should preach simply, and that they should not preach themselves, to use his own expression; for a much stronger reason would he have had a horror of seeing those of his disciples who are the last comers and the least zealous, taking glory to themselves for some most trivial works.

Further, the relations of one Conference to another

nave for their aim the recommendation of young men who leave their families to settle in a town where the Society exists. Nothing is more useful than this custom. How many young men there are who leave the paternal roof well-disposed to remain pure, chaste, religious! How many have promised it to their mothers, and have promised it to themselves! Nevertheless, no sooner are they settled in their new residence, than they lose all their pious habits, and sink into shameful excesses! The fault is doubtless in their passions, but it is more particularly in the isolation in which they find themselves from all pious companionship, from all Christian advice. Fortified by example, they would have maintained their rectitude; left to themselves, they fall miserably. To give to these young men, still practical Christians, a solid support, by means of good and pious associations, to form pure companionship for them within the bosom of the Conference, to bestow upon them encouragement, alas! too necessary, what service is not this to do for religion, for their families, and for themselves! Conferences are earnestly solicited to give their best attention to this, so that they should never omit to recommend to other Conferences such of their members as go away, and that they should give the most earnest welcome to young persons who come to them furnished with similar recommendations, and particularly that they may surround these young men with those safeguards and those precautions with which every father would wish to surround his son.

As to the poor who change their places of abode, it is likewise a very laudable custom to recommend them mutually. In this way the good may perhaps be finished in another place; only care must be taken that the removal of the poor be not made lightly and without a serious purpose, as is too often the case.

Nor should it be neglected to give recommendations to workmen who are making their *tour* of France, in order that they may be placed, as much as possible, in reputable houses, and with honest and Christian employers. The soldiers who are carried away by the conscription should also be objects of the attentions of Conferences, in order that Christian schools may be got up for them, where they may be taught to read and write, and particularly to love God.

2*

§ 1. ORGANIZATION OF CONFERENCES.

8.—The business of each Conference is administered by a Spiritual Director, a President, one or more Vice-Presidents, a Secretary, and a Treasurer, who constitute the *Council* of the Conference. There may be also in each Conference, if necessary, a Librarian, a Keeper of the Clothes Room, or other officers.

Article 8 enumerates the different officers of the Conferences, and it divides them into two categories—those who form the Council, to whom more particularly belongs the direction of the Conference, and those who fulfil certain accessory functions.

The Council of the Conference has, practically, a very great importance, particularly in such Conferences as are not under a Particular Council. It has to consider carefully the principal questions which belong to the business of the Conference, to prepare the matters which are to be submitted, in order to make its decisions clear and to shorten discussions. Although the Rule does not direct it, yet it is desirable that the meetings of the Council should be so frequent as that they should have an actual efficiency; but it is necessary to remark that, according to the spirit of the Rule, the Council has only to prepare the business for the Conference, to consider all projects carefully, and that it is for the Conference itself to decide, especially in the towns where a Particular Council is not in existence. To proceed otherwise would be to annul often the actual life of the Conference, and to take away all interest from its meetings.

9.—The President is elected by the Conference. The other officers are appointed by the President, with the advice of his Council. However, as is said further on, in the town where there is a Council of Direction, the Presidents, Vice-Presidents, and other officers of the Conferences, are appointed by the President of the Council. The Spiritual Director is always appointed by the Bishop or Archbishop of the Diocese.

Two cases may present themselves for the nomination of the President of a Conference; one, where there is but a single Conference in a town, and the other, where there is a Particular Council acting as a link between several Conferences.

In the first case, the Conference elects its President itself, and it cannot be otherwise. It is to be remarked, that this election is not made for a limited period, but for an indefinite time. This arrangement has, in some instances, been the subject of criticism on the part of some Conferences; they have feared that thereby there would be placed forever at the head of Conferences, officers whose intelligence or whose zeal would not meet every requirement; that, consequently, the progress of the Conference would be impeded through it, and that the poor would come to suffer by it. These fears have certainly some foundation, but the Council-General has always found them less serious than the inconveniences of an election. It is rare, in the first place, that an annual election, unless it be a mere matter of form, should not be a cause of a certain agitation, and in periods of dissension, political or otherwise, which may have to be passed through, that agitation may injure seriously the internal peace of the Conference. There might, besides, on account of these elections, be formed in the heart of an assembly, formerly the most tranquil, parties and little cabals. Preferences and antipathies might be engendered, and nothing could be more fatal to a work of charity. Then, is not the spirit of preservation and of permanence necessary for the direction of any work whatsoever; and if a President knows that he is nominated for one year only, can he so easily undertake works of long duration, *the Patronage of apprentices, the Holy Family*, etc.? Perhaps his successor may lead the Conference in another direction, and that would be then for him a reason for attempting nothing. Finally, in a Christian work, where the offices are charges and not distinctions, *onera, non munera*, if a president does really retard the progress of the work, are there not a thousand modes of charitably letting him know it? The experience of twenty years has many times proved that, without offending an honorable brother, it was possible to lead him thus to a retirement, which to him was but a rest long desired. For all these reasons, the Council-General has always opposed the system of annual elections, and, thanks to the affection which the Conferences have for its advice, this system is tending more and more to disappear.

The other officers of the Council are named in these Conferences by the President, with the advice of the Council. It appeared that this was the mode to preserve more unity in the direction, and not to multiply elections too much.

In the second case, that of several Conferences connected by a Particular Council, the nomination of the Presidents and Vice-Presidents of Conferences belongs to the President of that Council. Article 31 says that these appointments ought to be made by the President, with the advice of his Council. This arrangement has for its object to draw closer among the different Conferences the bonds of fraternity, and to maintain a unity of spirit by means of an appointment emanating from a common authority. It may occur, indeed, that in the heart of the same town, divergent tendencies may manifest themselves among different Conferences ; that one, for example, should incline towards the mode of proceeding of a Confraternity, another towards the usages of a mere relieving society; that this one would be too rigorous in the admission of its members, that too indulgent. The nomination of the Presidents of Conferences by the President of the Council wears away all these inequalities little by little and gently, and succeeds, through selections prudently arranged between the President and his Council, in blending these shades of difference in one common spirit,—that of the Society. Lastly, it is easier to study the peculiar fitness of such or such a candidate in a Council where the conversation is familiar, and where there are but few present, than in a Conference where there is greater publicity, and where every objection to the choice proposed may take the appearance of personality.

Finally, whatever may be the mode of appointment of the President, the importance of the selection cannot be too much insisted upon. While the President should never be in the Conference but as a kind of elder brother, the *primus inter pares*, experience proves that *what a President is, so is the Conference.* 'In order that a President should discharge his duties adequately, it should be considered not so much whether he enjoys a well-deserved position in the locality, or whether he is rich and generous, but much rather whether he possesses the personal qualities which are indispensable. Thus, above all, he must have *leisure* to occupy himself with the Conference, for an honorary presidency is always a barren one; he should have *zeal*, which often makes leisure; he should also have *energy* of mind as well as *maturity of judgment;* he should be animated with the *spirit* of the works, in order that he may know how to surmount the difficulties which the exercise of works of charity presents, in place of being frightened by them; he should have a *conciliatory spirit*, to prevent or to appease differences, and, in fine, that *piety* and *lively faith*, which know how to spread abroad, and which grow strong because they draw down God's blessings.

The constant usage of the Society (with some exceptions, which were almost always temporary), has been to confer the Presidentship of Conferences upon simple laymen. It is thus that the Society has been constituted, and has been approved of by the Holy See. But from the circumstance that the Presidency has not devolved upon ecclesiastics, it by no means follows that those among them who do us the honor of joining our ranks, not only as honorary members, but as active members, should not be received in them with the utmost gratitude. This is a point which the Circular of the 31st May treats of in the fullest manner.—(Page 250 of the *Manual.*)

10.—The President directs the business of the Conference, receives and submits propositions, calls meetings, if necessary, and watches over the execution of the rules and the decisions of the Society. In case of absence, he intrusts his duties to a Vice-President.

11.—The Secretary prepares the minutes of the meetings. He keeps a registry of the names, professions, and residences of the members, of the dates of their admission, and the names of those by whom they were proposed. He keeps an exact account of all the families visited. He makes diligent inquiry concerning those recommended for relief, so that the Conference may not, if possible, visit any family which is not worthy of its sympathy and support. He notes any changes that occur in the families visited, or in the members who visit them.

The President of a Conference is, in some sort, the soul of it; but he should not, however, absorb, through excess of zeal, the activity of the Conference in his own. It is well that he should watch over and superintend all that is done of importance, and that he should take his part in it, by his advice at least; but it is not desirable that he should overtask himself, and that he should take upon himself alone all the burden; for he would make, in some sort, his functions impossible to a successor somewhat more occupied, and he would destroy the zeal of the other members by thus always substituting his own for it.

When the President is absent, especially for some time, it should be understood that the Vice-President has all his powers, and *stands entirely in his place*. A Conference should never stand still for want of a member, and this would be the case if they did not venture to do any thing in the President's absence. It is therefore not alone his *right*, but it is *a conscientious duty* on the part of the Vice-President to supply fully the place of the President when absent or prevented from attending, in order that, when the latter shall return, he may not find that all has been languishing for want of him.

This remark concerns not only the Conferences alone;

it is applicable also, for stronger reasons, to Particular, Central, and Upper Councils, and above all, to the Council-General. In an undertaking, we must always have the undertaking in view, not the men.

The functions of the Secretary deserve special mention, notwithstanding that they are of less importance than those of the President; for if the President has all the direction upon his shoulders, the Secretary carries out the details. Upon his exactness or upon his negligence depends consequently a number of good things or of little irregularities.

Thus, when the Secretary is absent or comes late, the minutes are either not read at all, or are not read at the time fixed by the Rule, which is, in fact, the most convenient time. When he does not keep an exact note of the admission of members, of the adoption of families, of the names of visitors, the result is a grave irregularity; now, families long forgotten suffer from being neglected; now, there are others who receive double relief; and these inaccuracies greatly interfere with the regular business of the meetings.

Nothing would be more contrary to the usages of a society which is entirely voluntary, than finical habits, in imitation of the modes of proceedings of a public department, or of what is commonly called "red-tapeism;" thus the Council-General cannot do too much to lead away Conferences from every thing which would have this stamp upon it, and to recommend them to do every thing simply, without voluminous registers or multiplied forms; for otherwise the spirit of our dear Conferences would receive a serious injury from it. But simplicity in proceedings does not exclude order—quite the contrary; and precisely because things are done in a short time, they should be well arranged.

This is the spirit in which a Secretary ought to understand his duties. Thus, the register of the poor should always be kept up to the current time: opposite to the name and address of each family, and of the ordinary relief which they have been allowed, an entry should be made in a column of observations of the creditable circumstances which concern this family, the principal remarks made by the visitors, and of every assistance more than ordinary which has been granted to them. Such a register would occupy scarcely a quarter of an hour weekly to keep it up; and yet, it may be very useful for the proper guidance of the Conference, and especially for new visitors, who would find in it valuable information as to the poor intrusted them.

12.—The Treasurer has the care of the funds, and takes at each meeting an exact account of the receipts and disbursements.

This article is of greater utility than one would imagine at first, and Conferences are requested to follow it to the letter; on the one hand, because by keeping the state of the treasury each time under the eyes of the members, it induces each to proportion his demands to it resources, and on the other, because it guards against errors. Conferences, then, will do wisely not to depart from the terms of the weekly account being rendered by the Treasurer, as has sometimes been done for greater simplicity. But what is of more importance still, is never to fall into arrear with the purveyors. Besides that the price of provisions, and that of bread particularly, varies very often, and that if the Rule were departed from, it may give rise to disputes, it is dangerous for Conferences to allow debts to accumulate, and it may be, at some particular moment, a cause of great embarrassment. It is much better to pay ready money—it is the surest and the simplest way.

The investment of funds, when a Conference has received some sums of money which exceed the current expenditure, deserves also some attention. We do not speak of a perpetual investment of capital, which would be funded, and only the interest drawn, a course which would be very contrary to the spirit and to the traditions of the Society. We refer to those temporary investments, which, after a good lottery or a fruitful sermon, are made for some months until the winter, with the double view of procuring for the poor some additional comforts, and of assuring the preservation of the capital. Nothing positive can be said here upon it; but it seems to be prudent for Conferences to invest rather in public than in private securities, and to select those of fixed in preference to those of fluctuating values. High rate of interest is of much .ess consequence than complete security of the capital, and in critical times the money of the poor must be compromised as little as possible, and its recovery should always be prompt and easy. Finally, the investment of unemployed funds is the business of the Conference, and without its vote the Treasurer cannot do it, under the penalty of pledging his own moral responsibility.

Some Conferences have the habit of naming, at the Treasurer's request, a committe yearly for the verification of the accounts. This usage appears to be a very wise one, and Treasurers ought to adhere to it, as it protects their responsibility. Now-a-days, besides, it is of scarcely·less importance to prove that one is correct than to be so in fact.

13.—The Librarian collects instructive books adapted to the capacity of the persons' relieved by the Conference, and keeps an account of all books lent or bestowed.

14.—The keeper of the wardrobe collects the clothes for the poor, and keeps a regular account of them.

The importance of a library for the poor, recognized as it has been from the origin of the Society, is still greater to-day than formerly. The duties of a Librarian are then very serious, and the Conference should support in every way in their power the brother who devotes himself to it. It seems natural that the Librarian should be intrusted with the distribution at the meetings, of the *Little Lectures* (*Petites Lectures*), which it is so useful to have done continuously and regularly.

The wardrobe should be the object of the most particular care on the part of the Conferences; for the poor are as often in want of clothes as of food, and to obtain them one must often expend his trouble rather than his money. In the first place, the Conference must be often reminded of the wants of the wardrobe, always drawn upon, and a place above all others badly furnished; so, when an offer is made, we should avail ourselves of it quickly, and not let the occasion slip. When the clothing is brought together there is a good deal of time required for repairing, and it is here that the help of pious women is very precious for carrying out a crowd of details which men do not understand. In fine, it is necessary at times, as, for instance, in some towns, to organize searches in every house, to collect, with, it is to be understood, of course, the assent of the proprietors, all the old lumber which is lying by in garrets, from the old broken article of furniture or torn hangings, for which use would soon be found, to the pieces of linen so needful to the sick. The wardrobe may often cost very little, and yet be well filled. Then it is of immense service. For the sick, it provides old linen and changes; to the poor, who are in want of bedding, it affords the means of separating children of different sexes. What benefit is not a warm blanket, or a clean sheet, a dress, or a coat! It is often worth health, life itself, sometimes also the means of livelihood; for how many of the poor there are who cannot obtain situations for want of suitable clothing!

§ II ORDER OF THE MEETINGS.

15.—The Spiritual Director, or in his absence the President, opens each meeting with the prayer, *Veni Sancte Spiritus*, followed by the *Prayer*, with the *Ave Maria*, and *Invocation of St. Vincent de Paul*. A portion of some pious book selected by the Spiritual Director or President is then read. Each member is called upon in turn to perform this duty. The duty of prayer and pious reading should be discharged with the most serious attention; the spiritual good of the members being as much the object of the Society as the relief of the poor.

Prayer is an essential portion of the business of the meetings, and should never be omitted, as it brings to mind one of the distinctive characteristics of the Society.

The Society of St. Vincent de Paul is a Catholic work, and to draw down the blessings of God upon its labors, it should always endeavor to sanctify them. The prayer, too, should be gone through without human respect, upon bended knees; for he would very badly comprehend the humility which the service of the poor requires who would be unwilling to bend his knee in public before his God.

The pious reading should be made with attention, and should be neither too long nor too short; not too long, for fear of prolonging the meeting too much; nor too short, because the piety of the members should be nourished. The selection of the book from which the reading should be made belongs to the Spiritual Director; but of course the book ought to treat only of Christian and charitable subjects. In a certain old Conference, it has become a habit, that any member who in the course of his own reading meets with some passages worth remarking, and of a nature to edify his brothers, communicates them to the President, and with his assent reads them. This custom is a very good one, and deserves to be extended.

The works most used among the Conferences, for the pious reading, are the *Holy Gospels*, the *Imitation of Christ*, the *Introduction to a Devout Life*, the *Manual of Charity* by the Abbé Mullois, the *Lectures*, and *Counsels*. It is also very useful to read now and again, at least once a year, the whole of the Rules, the Circulars of the Council-General, and this Commentary.

16.—The Secretary reads the minutes of the preceding meeting. Each member is at liberty to make observations upon them.

The minutes ought to contain all that occurs of importance at the meetings, and particularly whatever may serve as a precedent; but they should be drawn up as simply and as shortly as is possible. They will thus be more to every one's taste.

17.—If there be occasion, the President announces the admission of candidates proposed at the preceding meeting, and invites their proposers to inform them of it.

18.—The President then announces the names of new candidates, should any such have been presented. Members who have any observations to make in relation to the candidates, communicate such in writing, or verbally, to the President, in the interval between the meeting at which the names are announced and that which follows next after. If no observations have been made, the admission of the member proposed takes place at the latter meeting. Each member should be careful not to introduce into the Society any one who will not edify his fellow-members, or be edified by them, and who will not endeavor to love his colleagues and the poor as brothers.

These two articles, which should be considered together, indicate the principal points in the *forms* to be followed in the admission of candidates. The points which they put most prominently forward are the following:

1st. The proposal ought to be made, in the first instance, to the President in private; for Article 18 lays it down that *it is the President who announces the names of the candidates who have been proposed.* The Circular of the 14th of July, 1841, explaining this passage, is to the following effect: "Moreover, we request that before proposing a candidate, those who propose him should never fail to confer on the matter with the President, who is specially charged with the direction and with the honor of the Conference;" and the Circular of the 1st of November, 1852, taking up the subject again, adds these reflections: "It is easy to understand how wise these directions are; for, if those who are proposing a candidate, in place of speaking of the matter in private with the President, began, as we see done too often, by proposing him publicly to the Conference, it would be much more difficult to prevent an admission which may be little to be desired. . . . If, on the contrary, the proposal is made always after an understanding with the President, it is to be presumed that it is done because it ought to be done."

2dly. Every member is free to make observations upon the candidate; but these observations ought not to be made during the meeting. In public, any discussion of a particular name, every hesitation, every question, would assume the appearance of a personality. If the habit were adopted of making observations in this manner, unless there were grave objections to make to the candidate, each one would ignore his own opinion, would hold his peace, only to give way to his regret apart from the others; whence it would result that, without the cordial assent of all, admissions would take place of some who should not be received, but whom one would shrink from objecting to publicly; whence, consequently, in the Conferences there would be absence of unanimity and of cordial co-operation, and sometimes even defections would take place.

Now, what should be the course to adopt if serious objections have been laid before the President? In such a case, the duty of the President is to have an explanation on the subject, in a free and perfectly cordial manner, with the proposing member, to induce him to withdraw the party proposed, if the opposition be serious and well founded. Nevertheless, it may occur that there would be differences upon that point between the President and the member who has made the proposal; in such a case the President will do well to consult with his Council, or even that of the Particular Council of the town, if there be one, and to fortify himself with their advice. It is then to be presumed that this mediatory opinion will be listened to, and that it will be easy to come to an understanding; but if, unfortunately, the difference of opinion should still continue, it can be put an end to only by a vote of the Conference—a final resort which is of very rare occurrence, and which ought always to be so.

But if no opposition arise, in that case, which is the most general, the President has not, according to Article 17, to call for a vote; he has simply to state that the proposed candidate has not been the subject of any observation, and to announce his admission. Open voting

would have grave inconveniences, and a ballot would be
a solemn proceeding little in accordance with the simple
habits of a Conference.

3dly. Besides the general condition which we have
enumerated, for the proposal of candidates, Article 18
mentions one especially, which is, perhaps, too little attended to: it says that *the member should edify his fellow-
members* AND BE EDIFIED BY THEM. This recommendation
is very important, because, if persons are induced to join
Conferences as members who do not find attractions in
them, who come there just to get through a duty, and because they are constrained to do it in some sort, zeal cannot but grow cold. "The first qualification" (as is very
wisely stated in the Circular of the 1st of November,
1847), "that a candidate ought then to possess in present-
ing himself for admission into a Conference, is to attach a
very high value to the prosperity of the Society, not as-
suredly through pride, but through a deep feeling of
gratitude towards God, who has raised up in our age this
plan, heretofore not thought of or not practised, of succoring the poor, and at the same time of making those
who visit them better."

4thly. At the commencement of the Society, when a
new member was admitted, it was usual for the President
to address an exhortation to him to explain the spirit of
our Conferences. Unfortunately this custom has not been
continued, and in consequence of the multiplicity of admissions, it was difficult to put it in practice. But it
cannot be too much insisted on that a kind welcome
should be given to new-comers, that they should not be
allowed to take their seats *incognito* in the midst of the
Conference, that certain of the members should be even
assigned to them, in order to lead them into the practical
business of our works; upon this their perseverance often
depends. More, the President gives to the new member
a copy of the *Manual* of the Society, and exhorts him to
make himself perfectly acquainted with it by frequent perusal of it. How much better, and more quickly, too,
would not the spirit of our Conferences spread among all
the members, if they were careful to read the Rules, the
Circulars, the facts connected with the Society! In
place of guessing at our customs and our rules, and sometimes arriving at a very incomplete notion of them, they

would become speedily and completely acquainted with them by such reading, which can never occupy much time.

Some Conferences have believed that there would be some advantage in giving to their members certificates to attest that they belonged to the Society.

This measure presents many inconveniences in a Society numerous and wide-spread as is that of St. Vincent de Paul. Besides the danger of the fabrication of false certificates, is not the still greater danger to be apprehended of seeing these certificates preserved during all their lifetime by men who may have abandoned their Conferences, and who would hawk about with a personal, interested view, these titles which had been too lightly conferred? Then, what are the advantages of these certificates? It is indeed not easy to say, for when a member travels or goes to another Conference, it is much preferable to furnish him with a letter from his President. It is at once simpler and safer.

5thly. It is well to call to mind that every member, upon entering the Society, can gain a Plenary Indulgence on the day of his admission, conformably to the Brief of the 10th January, 1845. It would be greatly to be desired that a member should never neglect this precious favor, which would certainly be for him the pledge of many other graces.

19.—The Treasurer announces the state of the funds and the amount of the collection made at the close of the preceding meeting, so that each member may proportion his demands for relief to the resources of the Conference.

The spirit of the Rule, as may be perceived by the 19th Article, is never to allow the expenses of the Conferences to get into arrear, but also not to lay up. It is in some sort the translation of that expression of our sacred writings: "If you have much, give abundantly; but if you have little, give a little, and the little thou hast, give willingly." The works of the Conferences being entirely optional, should be from day to day; besides, nothing is more Christian than to trust one's self to Providence, and to count upon its inexhaustible care, when the work is undertaken for God. To make a reserve, to have before us a disposable capital which we never touch, to lay out beforehand a budget as in a relief association, are proceedings essentially contrary to the spirit of our Society. When it has any thing and it finds out a real case of misery, it gives bountifully and with a generous heart; if it has nothing, it appeals to the charity of its members, to that of their friends, of the public; and up to this day, God has never permitted that this confidence should be deceived.

20.—Tickets available for relief in kind, and which vary according to the requirements of the poor, are then distributed. Each member is called upon in his turn by the President, and mentions aloud what he applies for, and for how many families. He gives, when called upon to do so, detailed information about these families. The relief should be punctually given to the poor at their residences, before the next meeting. But the members administering it may use their own discretion, both as to the precise time, number, and manner of their charitable visits, and also as to the best means of introducing into these families the love of religion and the practice of their duties. Should a member ask for any rules to guide his conduct, or for advice in difficult cases, he is heard with attention and kindness, and receives from the President and every other member such replies as their experience and charity suggest.

In some Conferences the power, not entirely absolute, but very extensive, of asking for his poor whatever relief tickets he may wish for, is left to each member. It would seem that this custom ought to be reformed; for the nat ural inclination which leads a man to be more moved with pity for the misery which comes directly under his own eye, the pleasure of giving to his poor more than on former occasions, a certain timidity, in fine, in the presence of reiterated importunities, easily lead members to swell their demands; and from this there necessarily results an injury to the equitable distribution of relief; for when each member fixes at his own discretion the allowances of his own poor, it is not possible that he should not make his demands with more or less ardor, according to his character, and that inequalities, much to be regretted, should not be established among the different families. It is, therefore, a prudent measure to intrust the classification of the poor to a Committee of Inquiry (or Visiting Committee), *always* composed of *the same* members. These members visit all the families who ask to be adopted, and they propose to the Conference their classification into certain categories, according to the degree of their necessities; then, once or oftener during each year, they revise the general list of the poor, after having made a special visit. The visitors are always listened to when defending the interests of their poor, and in case of disagreement the Conference decides.

Here another point presents itself, apparently a secondary one, but which, however, deserves attention. Is it well that members who have been absent from a meeting, should be able, in the interval between one meeting and another, to go to seek their relief tickets from the Treasurer?

The opinion of the Council-General has always been in the negative. They believe that the true interests of the poor, as well as that of the Conference itself, are opposed to this permission being conceded: the interests of the poor; for the members ceasing to have a positive necessity for coming to the Conference to get their relief tickets, would more easily free themselves from assiduous attendance at the meetings, and the weekly collection would be greatly affected by this, even although there was a collecting box at the Treasurer's, as has been sometimes proposed: the interests of the Conference; for, by absenting themselves frequently from the meetings, the members would certain ly in time lose the spirit of them, and the taste for them.

As to the mode of distribution pointed out by Article 20, it has necessarily been modified by the force of circumstances in such Conferences as are pretty numerous, as it would have taken up all the time of the meetings. Many Treasurers have adopted the habit of preparing beforehand the relief tickets of each member in an envelope, which is handed to him immediately; and in this manner the distribution is carried out immediately and without loss of time.

On the other hand, that which ought not to be laid aside, is the custom of asking from members detailed information upon the state of the families whom they visit. It is not, in point of fact, sufficient that religious improvement should take effect among the poor; it is necessary, for the general edification, that the Conference should know that it has been effected; it is necessary that it should be talked of, lest the new-comers, not hearing any thing said about it, should come to neglect it, and that even the old members should allow themselves to lose sight of it. Further, every member ought to announce immediately the death of any of his poor: the *De Profundis* is recited for his intention at the close of the meeting, and the Holy Sacrifice is offered up for him at a later period. If there be yet time, some members are appointed to accompany the body to the church, and to attend the funeral.

Nothing is more natural than the recommendation made by this paragraph. The families that are visited are all poor, and often in actual distress. To put off for a party of pleasure, for some affair of little importance, the *weekly* visit to be made to the poor, is an act of negligence deeply to be regretted, for those families often suffer from it. "We were looking out for you," say they sometimes to the visitors: "we were near being in want of food." If the visitors had not gone to see them, food would have failed them! This thought makes one shudder. In the world people sometimes complain of a dinner-party delayed, put off perhaps by a party of pleasure, or by an accident which will not occur again. But what then is this to a mother who has five or six children, and who puts them to bed fasting, without knowing whether she will have food for them on the next day? Let us think seriously of this cruel anxiety, and we will

never put off the visits through any fault of our own.
Besides, this exactness need not be mathematical, and
even, as a general rule, it would be wrong to give the
poor the habit of counting upon help at a fixed hour.
This would make them, as one may say, persons enjoying
an income, who would die of hunger if the rent were not
paid the very day it fell due, and who would become ac-
customed to making no effort to help themselves.

This paragraph recalls once again to visitors the aim of
the Society in its relations with the poor: it is to make
them better men and better Christians. In fact, this cannot be too much insisted upon, as without this the Society of St. Vincent de Paul would become a merely phil-
anthropic and purely human work, which, even humanly
speaking, is very barren and insufficient. The visitors
will have then to seek for every possible means of instructing the poor upon their duties, and of making them
thoroughly comprehend them. Sometimes it will be by
means of a good word addressed to the child, that they
will take the work in hand; sometimes by means of a
good book, an almanac, a little lecture (*petite lecture*), a
pious image, or a crucifix bestowed; at other times it will
be by means of some edifying reading, made for some
poor invalid, whom they will strive to instruct upon it.
The manner may be varied infinitely in the details, but at
the bottom it will never be accomplished but by a great
devotion to it, a great affection for it, and particularly by
means of prayer. Let us pray for the conversion of our
poor; let us obtain prayers for them from pious souls;
let us sacrifice something to this intention, and we may be
sure of success. It was thus that the Saints acted, and it
is one of the secrets of the conversions which they worked.

Of course, when a member consults the Conference
upon a case of difficulty, he should take care that no inconvenience can arise from making it public; if that be
so, he should consult the President privately.

21.—If relief in money, clothes, or books be
applied for, the grounds for such application
should be fully explained, and the Conference
votes. Should the case of distress be such that
a grant ot money is indispensable, and that

relief in kind will not answer instead, the members receiving the money must take special care
to watch diligently over the use made thereof.

This article expressly recalls a usage so well established, that it is scarcely necessary to state it, to wit:
that the distribution of relief in kind is the rule, and the
exception a grant of money. The reasons for this custom
are so obvious that it is useless to recall them.

Some Conferences have remarked that certain of their
members had a stronger tendency than the others to ask
for the extraordinary relief to which the 21st Article
refers. The result of this is, that, without their desiring
it, their poor are more favored than others. To remedy
this trifling abuse, the habit has been adopted of entering
the extraordinary relief which has been granted upon the
register of families, opposite to the names of the families
who had received it; so that the Conference is not again
put to the same expense for the same poor person without being fully aware of it.

22.—After the allocation of the different sorts
of relief, the members deliberate on the disposal of any situations they may be able to procure for the poor, on the plans for the relief of
the distressed, and on the families to be visited
by new members, or by those who wish to visit
more. No family can be admitted on the relief-
roll of the Society without a previous statement
of its wants, made either by the Secretary, or by
such other member as may have been appointed
by the President to collect information. Before
the Conference decides, every member has full
liberty to make any remarks upon the case he
may think useful.

The adoption of families should be the subject of very
serious attention on the part of the President and of the

Conference. It concerns, in fact, the prosperity and the honor of the Society that all abuses arising in this way should be avoided; that women still young, *particularly if they live by themselves*, should not be visited, and that every precaution should be taken to avoid even the appearance of a scandal. This principle has been laid down from the very commencement, and is again referred to in the preliminary considerations of the Rule; it has been pointed out above; but the more the Conferences are multiplied, the more is it indispensable to hold firmly to this. For poor are to be found everywhere; and when there is so great a choice among so much misery, we should connect ourselves only with those, the relief of whom is exempt from inconvenient circumstances, and cannot cause disedification.

Care must also be taken, particularly in large towns, to adopt only the poor who live in reputable houses. This rule may appear severe; but is it not a case to which the popular proverb may apply: "Charity well regulated begins at home?"

It is also fit that prudence should be used with regard to poor persons subject to grave faults—drunkards, persons of dissipated habits, or those living in a state of concubinage. Undoubtedly these poor people ought not to be entirely excluded, unless they are in the category of those of whom mention has been made above; but they must not be visited except in the desire to correct them, and but so long as there is hope of effecting that. Otherwise, if relief were still continued to them, after all advice had been exhausted, that would be a cause of scandal for the honest poor, and it would give them grounds for believing, although erroneously, that the Society attaches no value to good morals and honest conduct. There is in this, therefore, a wise middle course to be followed between too great strictness and too much indulgence; and by paying attention to it, success will be obtained.

Finally, care must be taken not to adopt such a number as would be too large, regard being had to the number of visitors. Otherwise, if the members take the charge of too many families, they would be led to visit them only in a passing way, to do no more for them than just to distribute alms, and to neglect spiritual relief,

4

which cannot be given but during visits of some duration
and entirely friendly in their character. This mode of
considering the matter is then very serious, and Confer
ences ought to lay down a rule for themselves, not to
adopt but just so many families as they can visit in a
Christian manner, and in the spirit of our holy patron.

But all is not done by adopting the poor: they must
have visitors allotted to them. This duty is the especial
task of the President; for some member may be suitable
for almost every family, and yet not succeed with certain
of the poor; he may be too timid or too harsh, too slow
or too hasty, for exceptional characters. To some of the
poor it is well to give a visitor who impresses them by the
gravity of his manner, and even by the importance of his
position; with others, on the contrary, success is to be
had only by gaining their confidence by force of perseverance and of long patience. There is, then, a double study
of the character of the visitors and of that of the poor, to
be made by the President, and he cannot attach too much
importance to it. With respect to the visitors, this labor
will be easy to the President, who meets them each week;
but with respect to the poor, it requires more trouble,
because their number is much more considerable. To
effect it, there are two means, between which the President can choose: either to make periodically, at least
once a year, the complete round of the families, or for
himself to pay the first visits, for some weeks, to the families newly adopted. Some Presidents have found the
leisure to carry out both plans at the same time; they
cannot be too much congratulated upon their doing so.

23.—Members leaving for a time, or for ever,
the place where the Conference is, give notice
to the President, who confides to others the
duties with which such members were charged.

The recommendations of this Article, although purely
of detail, possess a real importance. Thus, if a member
neglect to give intimation of his departure, his poor or his
works may be abandoned: if he forgets to acquaint the
President personally of it, or if he himself gives charge to
another member, either of his poor or of his works, the

allocation of the families by the President, of which mention has just been made, may be disturbed by it, or the works would not perhaps be intrusted to the brother to whom they would be most suited. In either case, the good order of the Conference would be disturbed by it, particularly if the circumstances were of frequent recurrence.

Let us add, that it is very well that the members who go away should draw up a detailed report upon the state of their poor, which would enable those who replaced them to understand better and sooner the characters, the necessities, and the misery of these poor. Some brothers have also, upon such occasions, the praiseworthy custom of giving to their Conferences a more considerable sum as alms, to represeht them in the collections in which, during their absence, they would not join, and to help the Conference in supporting its poor. This practice cannot be recommended too strongly.

24.—The Conference then considers any observations that may be made with a view to its interests, its increase, and the best use of its funds.

This part of the meeting ought not to be neglected, because the Conferences would readily degenerate and fall into monotony, were they to occupy themselves exclusively with material questions, and not to give a little time to such as are general. Here are two shoals to be shunned; the first—under pretext of being engaged upon more exalted interests, to allow themselves to get into speeches, into dissertations upon charity, into theoretical discussions, which would be quite opposed to the simplicity of our meetings; the second—to restrict themselves to what concerns the Conference exclusively. It cannot be too well remembered that the Society of St. Vincent de Paul is one, and, that this unity may be maintained, it is well that the Conferences should converse often about such things as occur of an edifying nature in other Conferences—that they should study to imitate them and to turn them to use, in order that they themselves may not fall into apathy and torpor. Thus, it is very suitable to

select that part of the meeting when it is most numerous,
to give an account to the Conference, either of whatever
has occurred of importance at the Particular Council of
the town, if there be one, or of the general advice con-
tained in the monthly *Bulletin* of the Society, or of the
interesting Reports of other Conferences.   It is also the
most opportune moment for reading the circulars of the
Council-General, a deep knowledge of which the members
are often so deficient in, and which is so useful.   Sometimes, all these documents are left to rest in the archives
of the Conference, which is the same as saying, in the
dust.   This is a very positive loss to the members.

It will be well, also, from time to time to have read, at
this period of the meeting, some profitable report upon
any special work of the Conference, with the view of
exciting interest, and of constantly stimulating zeal, which
is, alas! so ready to languish in every human work.

25.—At the close of the meeting, and before
the prayer, the Treasurer makes the collection,
to which each member contributes an offering
proportioned to his means, but always in secret.
Those who cannot spare time for the service of
the poor, try to increase the amount of their
pecuniary contributions.

The collection should not be made merely for *form's*
sake; it ought always to be done very seriously, and every
one is bound to examine himself before God, in his soul
and conscience, whether the sacrifice which he makes to
the poor is in proportion to his means.   Almsgiving, in
fact, is not to the Christian a simple counsel—it is a rigorous duty; and while it may be discharged otherwise than
by the collection at the Conference, and while a portion
(of the extent of which each one can alone be the judge)
ought to be reserved for other works, and especially for
those of his own parish, it is right that every member of
the Society of St. Vincent de Paul should, within the
bosom of his Conference, discharge this precept generous-
ly, liberally.   Otherwise, how could he ask of others, if
he has not commenced by being himself the first to give?

How, above all, can he ask of God to bless his labors, if he has not deserved that blessing by a truly adequate self-sacrifice?

The collection, then, ought to be a serious act, but it ought also to be a secret one; and nothing would be more opposed to the spirit of the Society than to stimulate its members to considerable donations by the attraction of publicity. Thus a newly-formed Conference had thought, with a very laudable intention, that the amount of its collections would be increased if they were made upon a plate, so as to allow each one's offering to be seen; and it sought the opinion of the Council-General upon it. The latter was unanimous in condemning this practice. Thus, too, other Conferences have sought to replace the weekly collection by an assessment laid upon the members, either according to a rate fixed beforehand, or according to each one's means. The Council-General has likewise been at all times opposed to a tendency in this direction. Besides the fear that an assessment upon a low scale would injure the prosperity of the treasury, and that an assessment at a high rate would keep away many good Christians of small means, yet zealous, it was most of all to be feared that the secrecy of the collection would be violated. In Conferences, there ought to be no differences of rank or fortune: this is one of the most certain causes of their success. Now, the less opulent should not be exposed to blush at the smallness of their alms, nor the more wealthy be tempted to grow proud of the superiority of their donations. If anywhere Christian equality should be preserved, it is in the presence of charity. Nevertheless, in some country Conferences, it has been permitted that gifts in kind may be made by members as their contribution to the collection. This departure, which yet does not prevent a collection according to rule, has been sanctioned by the nature of the circumstances.

The collection is intended for the use of the families visited, but the members should not neglect any other means that may present themselves of increasing the funds of the Conference.

At the commencement of the Society, the collections were almost the only resource of our Conferences; at present they still are one of the most considerable sources of revenue, and they amount, on an average, to the fourth of the total receipts. This continuance of resources personal to and furnished by the members themselves is a most happy sign; but, as the Rule says, the members should not neglect any other means that may offer of increasing the funds. These means vary according to localties and customs: here, it is a charity sermon; there, .otteries; elsewhere, bazaars or sales; almost everywhere subscriptions solicited, extraordinary donations procured; but what ought not to vary, are the principles which should govern the collection of these resources.

First, and above all, there must be a great zeal to keep up the treasury of the poor. Often there are numerous steps to take towards this end; there are refusals to be endured, sometimes even difficulties to be overcome. A member of the Society of St. Vincent de Paul ought not to allow himself to be daunted, provided, of course, that he has not exceeded the limits of propriety. When one sees closely the misery of so many families, when one's heart is sensibly affected by their privation, their nakedness, and more than all by their spiritual destitution, he ought not to let himself be checked by some refusals—he ought not to fear being importunate; the pleasure of solacing these miseries well deserves being purchased by some annoyances.

Yet if there must be zeal, in order not to lose through our own fault any occasion of increasing the patrimony of the poor, this zeal must not end in too human an attachment to material resources. In a Christian work, money never is more than a secondary thing: what effects more than all else is devotedness—desire for the salvation of souls. Whence arise two results: the first is, that if the treasury does not fill to the measure of our wishes, we must not be grieved at it, nor, above all, must we be discouraged, but on the contrary, we must persevere more than ever; the second is, that to get money we must never resort to modes which are not entirely of a Christian character. Nothing is, in fact, more fatal than to pursue a praiseworthy end by means which are not free from reproach, or to wish to accomplish a Christian work by ways contrary to Christianity. Consequently there should be no balls for Conferences, no theatrical representations; it is not necessary to state this; but there should not be even those lotteries, where cupidity is stimulated by the allurement of gain, where recourse is had to speculation to bring in funds; nor should any other means be adopted which are repugnant to simplicity or to humility. All ought to be modest, Christian, in order not to attract too much the eyes of the world, and not to alienate the blessings of God.

26.—The meeting closes with *the prayer to Saint Vincent de Paul*, and the prayers *Pro benefactoribus*, and *Sub tuum præsidium*.

The custom is established in some Conferences of reciting at the close of the meeting the prayer *for the use of the members of the Society*, which is to be found in the *Manual*, and at the end of the Rule. It cannot be doubted that this would be a source of graces for the Conferences, and it is desirable that as well the members individually, as the Conferences in a body, should recite this prayer frequently.

CHAPTER II.

OF PARTICULAR COUNCILS.

WHEN several Conferences are established in the same town, Article 4 states that they are to be united by a Particular Council. This is the place to examine the motives which have led to the creation of this institution and the spirit which should direct it. The details of its organization will appear further on.

The increase of members in the Conferences is certainly a very great benefit, and every member should labor actively towards it. Yet, there is a point beyond which this organization leads to serious inconveniences, namely, when the number of the members becomes too great. Then the meetings lose some of their cordiality, by be-

coming more formal, and some of their freedom, to prevent their falling into confusion and disorder. A Conference is then no longer a place of meeting for Christian
friends; it is an assemblage of men who deliberate
gravely; moreover, zeal greatly relaxes in the same
measure as numbers increase, since each one depends
upon the other, and individual interest diminishes. It is
then a great danger to a Conference to become too numerous; by it the spirit of simplicity, of fraternity, of
cordiality, may be wrecked. Thus it has been early considered as necessary for Conferences that have reached
this point, to divide themselves into several Conferences,
and experience has justified that opinion; but this division
was not intended to lead to a schism, nor even to an isolation, nor to an entire severance of the branches of the
original Conference. It is for this that provision has been
made by the organization of Particular Councils, which,
while letting the individuality of each Conference exist,
nevertheless combines the common strength of them all.
Experience has, moreover, proved the utility of the means
adopted.

Now, thanks to this combination, we have been enabled
to multiply the number of members in important towns
in a manner that could not have been expected. At
Paris, for example, while a Conference of 150 members
would have found almost insurmountable difficulties in
maintaining itself, there have been formed fifty Conferences, in which about two thousand members are included,
and by which they are drawn together by the attraction
of neighborhood, of parochial connections, and also by the
simplicity of meetings thus multiplied. In the less considerable towns a Conference could never have exceeded
the number of sixty or eighty members; divided into
three Conferences, it now has brought together more than
twice that number, and there are double the number of
poor visited, of funds collected, of good done. Here then
is a result which deserves to attract the attention of many
Conferences; but it will not be effected unless under the
double condition which the following articles develop,
namely—unity of direction in important matters, great
freedom of action for each Conference in the details of its
works.

The separation of one Conference into several Conferences is the most frequent case where there is occasion for the creation of a Particular Council; yet sometimes it happens in towns which are somewhat spread out, or in suburbs which are attached to them, that a second Conference is organized entirely outside of the first one. This does not make it the less necessary to bind these Conferences together by a common Council, but it should be remarked that the Council-General, before pronouncing the aggregation of the second Conference, always advises with the primitive Conference, in order to be well assured that they are acting harmoniously, and that the formation of a new centre is caused by charity, and not by such a rivalry as should be regretted.

In fine, we must observe that this institution, which was only applied at first to Conferences of the same town or of its immediate locality, has been extended recently to country Conferences. The boundary of the jurisdiction of the Particular Councils is in such case traced by the Council-General at the time of their institution; for this demarcation arises no longer from the nature of circumstances, and it varies according to the relations, the proximity, and the necessities of the Conferences grouped together. This innovation is very advantageous, since it is a protection against the dangers of isolation in Conferences scattered through the country, whose weakness makes it necessary that they more than all others should support one another.

27.—The *Particular Council* of a town is composed of a Spiritual Director, a President, Vice-President, Secretary, and Treasurer, of all the Spiritual Directors, Presidents, and Vice-Presidents of the Conferences of the town, and of the Spiritual Directors, Presidents, and Vice-Presidents of Special Works in which all are interested.

The composition of Particular Councils has been conceived, as may be readily seen, in the double thought indicated above, of unity of direction, and of free action of the Conferences for their works. Thus, there is at the

head a board, the members of which need not be attached
to any Conference, an I which ought necessarily to tend to
encourage them all in an equal degree; then, besides this
board, there are the Presidents and Vice-Presidents of
each Conference, and the Presidents and Vice-Presidents
of the Special Works.   All interests then are protected
there, in order that the decisions arrived at may be accepted more freely by all; all the works are there present,
in order that the absence of any one may not involuntarily
cause its interests to be postponed.

With regard to the *special* works, as the Rule calls them,
and which it would be more correct to call *general works*,
they are those which, for their full development, require
the common concurrence of all the Conferences.   These
works alone are represented in the Particular Councils,
and not the works of this or that Conference which have
the President of the Conference for their natural guardian.

It is well to note, in passing, that when the article speaks
of a *Vice-President*, here as in many other articles, that
does not prevent more being named if there be a real necessity for them; so also as to Vice-Secretaries and Vice-
Treasurers.   Nevertheless, it would be very much opposed
to the spirit of the Society to multiply beyond what is
necessary, the number of officers, in order to foster self-
love and vanity.

28.—The *Particular Council* is charged with
those works and important measures which interest all the Conferences of the town.

This article determines plainly the functions of Particular Councils.   Thus, if the matter in question be concerning a work entirely of detail, or the internal arrangements
of the relief in a Conference, the Particular Council has
nothing to do with it, since that does not affect all the
Conferences of the town.   But if, on the contrary, it is a
question of regulation, which concerns the Society at
large—if it is a measure, the result of which will not be
confined to the Conferences of the town, but may extend
over all the others, it does not lie, strictly speaking, with
the Particular Council to come to a decision on the matter;
it has only to offer advice, leaving it to the Council-General to give a definite solution.   But when a question

arises upon a measure that interests *all* the Conferences of the town, and which *concerns them only*, it is then that the action of the Particular Council comes into operation, and that it has the right to adopt positive decisions. Without entering into the detail of these measures, it is certain that they are of frequent occurrence. Thus, where new Conferences are formed, it is for the Particular Council to fix their limits. When some important works are proposed, it is for it to decide upon whether there is occasion for them, how they should be proceeded with, etc. When a Conference departs from the rule, it is for the Particular Council to remind the Conference of the rule, and by its advice to lead back to its observance.

29.—It decides on the allocation of the common fund. This fund is maintained by all donations not made expressly to any of the Conferences, collections made at the general meetings of the town, and by the contributions which the Presidents bring to the Council in the names of their respective Conferences. This fund is intended to meet the expenses of the special works of the town, and to sustain the poorer Conferences.

The administration of the common funds of the Conferences is one of the functions of the Particular Council. These funds are destined, as the article says, to meet the works of the town and to support the poorer Conferences. This destination shows all their utility, and proves how valuable they are. Misery never is, in fact, distributed equally among the different quarters of a town, and it is very right that the more abundant resources of the better-circumstanced Conferences should aid the distress of the others. It is one of the most Christian applications of the true charity which should animate the members of the Society, and one of the most positive proofs that they all act but with one heart and one soul. This is the place to add that the funds of the Particular Council, as well as those of the Conferences, ought always to be employed upon the works of the Society. "We have been asked," says the Circular of December 1st, 1842, "if it be permissible to apply some of the funds received as donations or through the collections at Conferences, to any other charitable purpose than the works specially adopted by them. It appeared to us that this ought not to be done; that it would be, firstly, to misunderstand the intentions of the donors; that, secondly, such a latitude would have as a result, to embarrass considerably the works which we have undertaken. By wishing to do every thing, we would end, in fact, by doing nothing. A charitable society, which does not know how to limit itself, is soon exhausted. Because we have selected certain works, we have not entered upon an engagement to devote ourselves to all. Pardon me, Sir and dear Brother, if in this I appear to wish to restrain the effects of your zeal; but we must be wise with soberness, and it is to make your efforts more efficacious and more lasting, that I hazard these counsels of a prudence which may seem to be timid."

The supply of the funds of the Council presented a double difficulty: of drawing too much to itself, or of being insufficient. If the resources of the Conferences had been too much concentrated in the common fund, their zeal in collecting funds would certainly have been diminished. It is, perhaps, a weakness to wish to expend by our own hand, or through our Conference, the money which we have procured, and to put so much the more ardor in its collection, as we shall have greater share in its distribution; but this weakness is too natural to man that it should not be taken into account. If, on the other hand, too moderate resources had been destined for it, the common fund would have been without an object. It appears that the Rule goes safely between these two dangers.

Thus, every Conference is exclusively proprietor of the funds which it receives by weekly collections; by subscriptions; by donations made to it; by the local resources which it procures within its own limits, and which vary according to local customs.

The Council centralizes the donations made to the Society in the town, and not made to this or that Conference, the funds arising from lotteries, general collections organized not in a single parish, but in the entire town, the contributions of honorary members (Art. 55), the collections made at the general meetings of the town, and the offerings of each Conference. Besides, it is to be remarked that this limitation is necessarily, to a small extent, somewhat variable and elastic, and that, in the spirit of the Society, there ought to be made under this head, between the funds of the Council and those of the Conferences, certain concessions according to the exigencies of the occasion. Further, the offerings of each Conference are now fixed generally at a certain per centage upon their funds. It seemed useless, in fact, to renew a vote upon this matter at every meeting of the Conference. At Paris the Conferences vote the tenth of their funds, and this allocation is sufficient on account of their number; in other towns, a different proportion has necessarily been adopted.

30.—The Spiritual Director, President, Vice-President, Secretary, and Treasurer, constitute the ordinary Council, to which belongs the direction of the ordinary business.

Just as in simple Conferences, this council is of great importance; not only does it prepare the subjects for deliberation, and thus shorten them, but it also expedites a crowd of small details, in which the President is very glad to receive advice, but which are not worth calling an extraordinary meeting for. So that nothing is done precipitately, and nevertheless small matters, which are the most numerous, are not protracted indefinitely. This is a very important point; for in works of charity, if it be of consequence to do them well, it is also necessary to do them quickly.

31.—The President is appointed by the Council, with the advice of the Conferences. On the first occasion he is appointed by all the Conferences together. The President appoints the Presidents and the Vice-Presidents of Conferences and of Special Works, as well as the Vice-President, the Secretary, and the Treasurer of

5

the Particular Council, taking the advice of his
Council upon all these appointments.

This article clearly defines the occasions and the manner
of nomination of the different officers and members of the
Particular Council. One question only has been raised,
viz., can the Council nominate the President, *after getting
the advice of the Conferences, but still contrary to that
advice?*—and can the President nominate the officers
whom he is charged with selecting, *after the advice of his
Council, but still contrary to that advice?* The Council-
General being consulted upon this point, were of opinion
that *in principle* the Particular Council, as well as the
President, could proceed with the nominations which belong to them; but that, in a work of charity, we must adhere less to a cold interpretation of the text, than to the
nature of the circumstances. Now, in fact, it is certain
that a Council could not impose a President upon the
Conferences of a town *in spite of them*, and that a President could not impose upon his Council members whom
the majority of that Council would *formally* reject. Here
charity solves the difficulty, as also it will prevent its
being raised; for, in order that good may be possible,
there must be an intimate union among all; and a great
danger to the Society would manifest itself upon the day
when any in it would wish to act in virtue of rights and
of prerogatives, and not rather through a mild firmness.

32.—The President of the Particular Council
directs its proceedings, receives and submits
propositions, and calls meetings when necessary.
He presides at the general meetings of the district.

The Rule does not define the time of meeting of the
Particular Councils; and it could not do so, for what would
suit in one town is often not expedient in another; thus,
at Paris a necessity has been felt for the Particular Council of the city to assemble every eight days; and these
repeated meetings have answered very well. In other
places, on the contrary, fortnightly or monthly meetings
are amply sufficient. The necessities of each town must,

then, be taken into account; but it is desirable that the meetings should not be held at a greater interval than a month, since a Council, to be real, must be active.

33.—The Secretary prepares the minutes of the meetings of the Council. He keeps a regis ter of the names, Christian names, professions, and residences of the members of all the Con- ferences of the town, with the dates of their admission, and the names of their proposers. He also registers the native places of those who have not a fixed domicile in the town.

The points of detail which the 33d Article enumerates ought to be carefully observed; and experience has proved that none of these particulars is superfluous. Secretaries of Particular Councils ought, then, to endeavor to take care of this matter, as should Secretaries of Conferences apply themselves to keeping up the lists of members and those of the poor.

34.—The Treasurer has charge of the common fund of the town.

It follows that it is to the Council that he accounts. It is well that, as in the Conferences, these accounts should be audited yearly.

35.—The Conferences are represented in the Particular Council by their Spiritual Directors, Presidents, and Vice-Presidents. The Spiritual Directors, President, and Vice-Presidents of *Spe- cial Works* appear there to watch over the inter- ests of these works. Each makes reports when invited to do so by the President of the Council.

There is nothing to point out here but the final arrange- ment in this article, and to insist upon the usefulness of Reports being made frequently to the Council upon the state of the Conferences and of the works. These reports, although they ought always to be made in a simple style, yet keep interest heartily alive; they prevent meetings from being dull or monotonous; they afford the occasion to Councils to probe to the quick the Conferences and the works of the town, to give advice, to rectify usages that are defective, to extend such as are useful, and thus to form, by the force of example alone, a unity of heart and of mind among the different Conferences.

CHAPTER III.

THE COUNCIL-GENERAL.

36.—The Council-General is composed of a President, Vice-President, Secretary, Treasurer, and of several Councillors.

37.—The Council-General is the bond of all the Conferences—it maintains the unity of the Society. It labors for whatever can promote its prosperity. In this respect it adopts the course which it judges most useful.

The Council-General is the centre of the entire Society. It aggregates Conferences, institutes the Councils of different degrees, fixes their limits, pronounces, if there be occasion, and in serious cases, the dissolution of Conferences and of Councils, adopts general decisions which extend to the whole Society, interprets or modifies the General Rule, as occasions arise, and directs all the Conferences by its correspondence, its circulars, and the *Bulletin*. Its exist-.nce goes back to the origin of the Society, so soon as there were several Conferences; and its action has been successively developed according as the general interests of the work have increased and have become of greater importance. The Circular of December, 1837 (pages 160 to 162 of the *Manual*), gives the history of it. The Rule devotes a chapter to its organization. [See, with regard to the enumeration of the officers, the remark inserted at Article 27.]

38.—It decides upon the allocation of the central fund. This fund is maintained by donations made to the Society, by collections made at the general meetings of the Society, and by contributions from the Conferences and Councils towards the general expenses of the Society.

Notwithstanding the strictest economy, it is not possible that the Society should not have some general expenses; every individual Conference, every Council, necessarily has some; the Council-General, charged with representing the whole Society, with corresponding with its different branches spread all over the world, so to speak, could not escape this obligation, and of course feels it in a still stronger degree. Whence the creation of a central treasury; but it is of the very essence of our work to restrain these expenses to what is strictly necessary, to do every thing with simplicity, and, consequently, with economy, and to be sacredly avaricious of the money of the poor in respect to every thing which does not go *directly* to their relief. The spirit of the Society would be deeply injured, and its success, perhaps, be compromised, on the day when these habits would be deviated from.

The 38th Article places the annual offerings of each Conference and of each Council among the resources of the treasury of the Council-General. It is but just that the Conferences of Paris should not bear alone such expenses as relate to the whole Society, and that *each* Conference, having its share in the general expenditure, should have its share, too, in the means of providing for it. Some Conferences have of themselves decided that they would adopt, as the base of their annual contribution, the hundredth part of their receipts; but whatever may be the gratitude of the Council-General for that decision, on this subject nothing is prescribed by the Rule, nor even demanded by the Council-General; these gifts are entirely optional, and it appears that the more they are spontaneous, the more valuable they become.

Moreover, the purpose of the treasury of the Council-General is not merely to defray the expenses of correspondence and of administration. It ought, especially, to come to the aid of poor Conferences, for which temporary assistance is eminently useful. Every year the Council-General allocates grants, which are unfortunately insufficient, either to Conferences which are organized in poor localities, and to which a small remittance of money is a valuable encouragement, or to those which, some time in existence, are assailed by greater necessity. Thus, many Conferences have been supported, upheld, preserved perhaps from the inefficiency into which they were about to fall. Alone, they would have succumbed; but, feeling themselves sustained, they have regained courage, and they have imparted it to the poor whom they relieved, and to the rich who could give them co-operation.

But occasions arise of so serious a nature, that the treasury of the Council-General, which is always very inconsiderable, cannot succeed in affording a remedy for them. Thus, after the inundations of the Rhone and of the Loire, during the famine in Ireland and that in German Lorraine, the wretchedness became of such proportions that the united efforts of all the Conferences were required to bring some remedy for the evil. In such circumstances the Council-General first gives its own little contribution, and then makes an appeal to the Conferences—either a general appeal, if the misery be excessive, or one limited to certain countries, if the misery be confined within a certain radius. There is cause to thank our good God for the result of these appeals, for they have been always received in the most charitable and most fraternal manner.

Finally, these general calls made upon the Conferences should be confined to very rare cases; for these exceptional means can be had recourse to profitably only so long as they are used with extreme discretion. Further, they ought to be made by the Council-General *only*. Otherwise, there would no longer be any regularity as to them, and each being judge of the occasion of the calls, the result of this would be such a multiplicity of them that irregularity would ensue.

The consequence of this is (and perhaps it is not useless

to recall it to mind) that no Conference ought, *of its own accord and by itself*, to transmit lottery tickets, circulars for subscriptions, requests for money, to the Conferences at large. In the district of a Particular, Central, or Superior Council, it can be done within that circumscription *with the assent of that Council;* but outside that circumscription a general application can be made only through the intervention of the Council-General. This is at once the way to make important subscriptions succeed, and to prevent those being attempted which are not of that nature.

39.—The members of the Council-General are nominated by the President, with the advice of the Council.

According to an old custom, confirmed by a decision of the Council-General, under date of November 24th, 1851, it is for the Council-General to decide if there be occasion to nominate new members. When that decision is in the affirmative, the President-General, after having taken the advice of the Council, nominates the new members of the Council. (See on this subject the commentary given upon Article 31. The same principles are applicable here.)

No figure has been fixed for the number of members of the Council, since the necessity may vary according to circumstances, and with the increase of the Society it may be useful to call upon more fellow-workmen; but, according to the spirit of the Rule, no more than the number of members that is really necessary should be introduced into the Council. It has always appeared that these duties ought to be active, and not simply honorary, and that if the members were too numerous, it would be less easy to preserve the necessary unity of purpose and of direction. In fact, the number of the members of the Council-General has been, for many years, between twenty and twenty-five.

The members of the Council-General are chosen, as a general rule, from among the Presidents or members of Conferences who have rendered most services to the Society, and who can devote most time and intelligence to the general interests; yet the Council-General has always reserved to itself the liberty of calling into its body persons remarkable by reason of their piety and their

love of good works, persons who honor our work by
coming to give their co-operation to it. But, it should be
understood, that such a case ought to be a very rare exception, being caused by circumstances and by the qualities of the future members of the Council.

40.—When a President-General of the Society
is to be nominated, the Council-General is convened by the Vice-President. This meeting is
preparatory, its sole business being to deliberate
as to the person who may be considered eligible
for the office. If the former President be living,
he is requested to designate some person whom
he thinks it would be proper to select.

When the Council has deliberated upon one
or more names, it adjourns for two months. In
the interval, the proceedings of this preparatory
meeting are made known to the Presidents of
the Particular Councils, who consult their colleagues, and to the Presidents of the Conferences, who consult their respective Councils, or
even the Conferences over which they preside ;
all the Presidents transmit their opinions to the
Council-General, and according to these opinions the Council-General makes the election ; an
exact minute of which is recorded. While the
election is pending, all the members of the Society offer up, either in private or in their meetings, as a special prayer to God, the *Veni Cre-
tor*, that His spirit may enlighten them in the
choice they are about to make.

The article indicates sufficiently the mode of election of
the President-General, and there is no necessity for going

into details. The important point is, to remind t10 Con ferences of the necessity for prayer while that selection is being carried out; for that election is always a serious event in the Society, and the grace of God cannot be too much implored that a choice beneficial to the work may be made, and that the candidate nominated may be worthy of the laborious charge to which he is called.

41.—The President-General convokes extra-ordinary meetings, and presides both in the Council-General and in all general meetings.

42.—The Secretary-General keeps a register of the names, Christian names, professions, residences, and dates of admission of the members; also of the officers of the Councils or Conferences, and of the places, days, and hours of their meetings. He prepares the minutes of the meetings of the Council-General, and of general meetings. He draws up an annual report on the state of the works of the Society. He is charged with the general correspondence with the Presidents or Secretaries of the several Councils or Conferences. He keeps the archives of the Society.

Of course the members, of whom the Secretary-General keeps the list, are those of the Conferences in Paris; a General Register of all the members of the Society would be actually impossible, and it has never been thought of.

It should be mentioned that the correspondence ought to be arranged with the President-General, or the Vice-Presidents-General, delegated for that duty; the custom has, moreover, been introduced, that all the letters written in the name of the Council-General should be signed by two members, in order that nothing contrary to the spirit or to the usages of the Society should, through mistake, find its way into them.

43.—The Treasurer-General has charge of the funds. He keeps a regular account of the receipts and disbursements, and submits his accounts to the Council-General.

44.—If the President-General himself cannot preside at the Council of Paris, he appoints a member of the Council-General to do so. He also, on the recommendation of the Secretary-General, appoints several members of the Council-General to the office of Vice-Secretaries.

Article 44 lays down a useful principle, one applicable in all cases where two Councils—as a General Council and Particular Council, an Upper Council and a Particular Council, a Central Council and a Particular Council, etc. —are together in the same town; namely, that a member of the Council which is the highest in authority— either the President or a member delegated *ad hoc* by the President—should always be the one to preside in the Council of lower rank. Undoubtedly, bickerings and discussions about pre-eminence are little to be apprehended in an assemblage for charitable purposes; but it would be so disagreeable to have them raised that they must be avoided as much as possible, and the concentration of the Presidentship of the two Councils in the same person is one of the most effectual means of preventing discussions and chances of offence being taken.

CHAPTER IV.

GENERAL MEETINGS.

SOMETHING has been said already of General Meetings and of their utility :—this is the time to study their spirit and details more closely.

General meetings are the assembling together of many Conferences, where several of them exist in the same town, or even the assembling together of the active and honorary members of the sole Conference of a town. This point deserves to be well determined; for many times some isolated Conferences have thought that they could not hold general meetings unless by uniting themselves to some Conferences of the neighboring localities, and that it would be impossible for them to hold general meetings by themselves alone. This notion is quite opposed to the practice of the Society, which regards as a general meeting every more formal assembly, where, in the presence of the members, both active and honorary, and of the benefactors of the Conference, an account is given of the good carried out, and of that which is contemplated. It would, moreover, be very unfortunate that it should be so: for, by omitting the general meeting, the Mass of the festival days would, perhaps, be omitted, the members would cease to meet for the purpose of praying together, so as to warm each other in piety; or, at least, if they did not give up the pious meetings, they would lose the Plenary Indulgences of the four Festivals of the Society, which cannot be obtained but upon the double condition of communion and of assisting at the general meeting. (Brief of January 10th, 1845).—(See the Circular of November 1st, 1849, pages 327 to 329 of the *Manual*.)

Now, it is beyond doubt that holding the four meetings presents some difficulties in small towns; that it is not easy to collect together four times a year some members of the clergy, some persons strangers to the daily works of the Conferences, in order to occupy them with results of little consequence; for this reason the Council-General has not ceased, for many years past, to recommend to neighboring Conferences to make arrangements for holding general meetings in common: sometimes in one town, sometimes in another; it is partly for this reason, also, that it insists upon the organization of Central Councils by means of which this part of our Rule can be more easily put into operation.

General meetings are, in fact, very useful for reviving zeal; they interest the honorary members and the benefactors in the work sustained by their co-operation; they afford the opportunity of speaking to them of the poor, and of obtaining for the poor more powerful assistance; they form, too, for the active members an occasion for reviewing the whole of their works, and of seeing how they could be improved. In every point of view they are, then, useful, and in towns where there are many Conferences they are necessary in order to keep up mutual relations. Yet care must be taken that they do not degenerate into mere formal meetings, and be made an occasion for speeches and eloquent displays, but that they remain what they ought always to be, a family meeting, somewhat more numerous than is usual, but ever humble, Christian, and full of simplicity.

The Council-General has been often asked if ladies ought to be invited to the general meetings. Notwithstanding local reasons which have a certain weight, the Council-General has always answered in the negative, since, to this step, which would be free from obstacles in some towns, there may be some objections in other more considerable places, and the precedent once established, it would be difficult not to allow it to extend itself continually, even until it would become the rule.

45.—General meetings are held every year, on the 8th of December, the Feast of the Immaculate Conception of the Blessed Virgin; on the first Sunday of Lent; on the Sunday of the Good Shepherd (the anniversary of the translation of the relics of Saint Vincent de Paul): and on the 19th of July, the Feast of this our patron Saint. The President is empowered, moreover, to call extraordinary general meetings.

The dates fixed by the rule for the general meeting ought to be scrupulously observed; and it would be very much to be regretted if isolated Conferences believed they could alter them. Is it not, in fact, touching to think that at the same periods all the members of the Society of St. Vincent de Paul are assembled to speak of God, of their poor, and of their own sanctification? Are there not graces attached to this simultaneousness of prayers and of action? Yet it should be observed that the days indicated are not imperatively required by the Brief of January 10th, 1845, which allows some days' latitude for holding the general meetings, so as to gain the indulgence: *atque cœtui generali qui hisce temporibus habetur interfuerint.* It would, in fact, often be difficult to hold the meeting actually on the appointed day.

46.—The general meetings, like the Conferences, open with prayer and pious reading.

It is very useful to observe this arrangement, and it should never be departed from, on any pretext, lest the general meetings may lose the mark of a Christian assembly. With this motive, the Council-General has always been of opinion, that if it is often useful to invite persons who are strangers to the Society, whether for the purpose of removing some prejudices, or of obtaining their co-operation, the prayer and pious reading should never, out of consideration to them, be omitted. If those persons have the misfortune of being such indifferent Christians as to be annoyed at this being done, it is much better not to invite them. It is of little consequence that our meetings should be brilliant; but it is of very great consequence that they should preserve their religious character.

47.—The Secretary having first read the minutes of the preceding meeting, calls aloud the members admitted into the different Conferences since the last general meeting, and whose names

6

have been remitted to him for this purpose by the different Presidents. These members rise — the Secretary presents them to the Society and the President, who addresses them in a few words.

The actual presentation of the members to the meeting and to the President, has become almost impossible in practice at pretty numerous general meetings. Disorder and confusion would result from carrying it out. But when the meeting is not very great, it is well to keep to this custom, which is a good proof of the spirit of brotherhood, and which is very old.

48.—The Presidents of Conferences report on the state of their Conferences. A summary abstract of each report, containing the changes of members and of poor families, the total receipts, with the amount and items of the expenditure, is deposited in the hands of the Secretary.

This article cannot now be followed literally, except at general meetings where few Conferences come together: it would, in fact, be impossible that ten or twelve Presidents, sometimes even forty or fifty, should come forward in succession to give accounts of the works of their Conferences; it is then necessary that they should forward to the Secretary their notes upon the material points, and that the latter, either himself or through another member, should draw up a complete statement.

Further, whatever may be the form of the report, an essential point is that it should contain edifying facts, of a nature to excite zeal, and above all, that it should not be a panegyric of the Society. The praises which a work receives outside, are often the cause of great danger to it; but the panegyrics which it pronounces on itself, are proof that the Christian spirit has departed from it.

49.—The Secretary then reads letters from those Conferences which have not been able to send a representative to the meeting. He also reads extracts of any other letters which may interest the Society.

50.—The President then announces the measures taken by the Council of Direction for the good of the Society, and, if necessary, solicits the advice of the meeting.

The last part of the article is entirely optional, as the expression "*if necessary*" shows. In fact, general meetings having become very numerous, it would be difficult now to take their opinions, in the large towns more especially.

51.—The President, or any member of the Society invited by him, addresses the meeting in a few words of Christian and charitable exhortation.

The address here referred to, and which occurs sometimes at the commencement, sometimes at the close of the meetings, should be short, simple, and practical. It should not be either a theoretical discussion, since such matter is not the purpose of the Society; or a sermon, since that would be misplaced in the mouth of a layman. But if it is made so as to present the special wants of the Society, if it points out carefully the difficulties to avoid in this or that work, if it excites to zeal and to devotion, it may really contribute to the charitable life of the Conferences.

The Society considers itself fortunate when persons eminent for their character, their virtue, and their knowledge, are good enough to be present upon the invitation of the President at the general meeting, and to close it with some edifying remarks.

The general meetings are, as much as possible, held under the presidency of a bishop or parish priest, or of a clergyman remarkable for his piety and virtues. It is an honor and a happiness for the disciples of St. Vincent de Paul to be able to relate their feeble labors to their fathers in the faith and their guides in Christian works; and, when, against their will, they are deprived of such presence, their meetings lose the greatest part of their charm and of their interest.

The rule is, and this rule justifies itself too well to need having it insisted upon, that the places of honor at the meeting belong, of right, to the clergy, and that the lay President does no more than direct the arrangement of the meeting. It is to their lordships the bishops, when they are so good as to come among us, or to the priests whom they select as their substitutes, that the first places, above the lay Council, belong. This is a testimony, a very trifling, but a very legitimate one, which Christians owe to the ministers of God, and which should never be forgotten.—(See the Circular of May 31st, 1846, page 252 of the *Manual.*)

52.—After the collection and usual prayers, the meeting closes.

CHAPTER V.

THE DIFFERENT MEMBERS OF THE SOCIETY.

53.—Besides its active members, the Society has corresponding members, honorary members, and subscribers.

Another category of members has, for many years past, been added to those stated in the Rule : this is that of the *Aspirant Members.* These members are chosen among young men under eighteen years of age; sometimes they are joined to ordinary Conferences, whose labors they take part in under the direction of the elder members;

sometimes they are sufficiently numerous to be organized into Special Conferences, either in Catechism classes for adults (*Catéchismes de persévérance*), or in Christian Colleges or Seminaries. This institution, whatever may be the mode adopted, is very valuable; besides that it gives useful auxiliaries to the Conferences, and provides for recruiting them among young people growing up, it trains the young to the spirit of charity and of zeal, and suggests to them the very natural desire of becoming active members of Conferences when they shall have arrived at the age to do so. The Brief of January 10th, 1845, makes aspirant members participators in the Indulgences of the Society, and the Council-General has published a special instruction for the Conferences of Colleges and Institutions.—(See the BULLETIN for May, 1853, page 132, and the following pages.)

54.—A member changing his residence and going to a place where there is no Conference of Saint Vincent de Paul, does not thereby cease to belong to the Society;—he becomes a *Corresponding Member;* he puts himself in communication with the Conference or Conferences of the town of his diocese nearest to his residence, and corresponds with the Secretary of the Council or of the Conference of that town. Should there be no Conference in his diocese, he corresponds with the Secretary-General.

The Circular of November 1st, 1849, comments upon this article as follows (page 333 of the *Manual*):
" It is time to turn this article, hitherto a dead letter, so to speak, into actual practice. But the great difficulty consists in drawing closely together the relations between the corresponding members and the Conferences, and in giving something to do to these members as well as to the Conferences, in order to keep up the relations once they have been opened. Now, if every isolated member communicated, as the Rule points out, with the Conference of

his diocese (or, in countries where that organization exists, with the Upper or the Central Council), if he were received in the capacity of *corresponding member*, if he sent his offering to it regularly, and received in return the funds necessary for succoring, *in the name of the Conference*, the poor of the locality where he is living; if he transmitted, at certain periods, a report upon the families —upon their moral and material condition—much advantage would result from it to all parties; in the first place, to the corresponding members, who, in this organization, would recover the incentive of association, of which they were deprived, and in this way would escape from the isolation in which they were in regard to the Society; to the Conferences in the neighborhood, who would have the germ of a body of devoted members ready to dispose of through the country lottery-tickets and collection circulars, to circulate reports, almanacs, and good books; to the entire Society, which, by becoming better known, would spread itself more easily in a great number of small towns, of extensive hamlets, and even of villages; in fine, to the poor in the country, who would receive some additional succor, and, what is more important, would obtain some more persons to serve them.

" If this plan be not adopted, there is a more simple way of arriving at the same end. but a less perfect one, as it seems to me.   You have doubtless remarked, Sir and dear Brother, in the Brief of January 10th, 1845, a very striking arrangement: the permission accorded to isolated members of gaining the Indulgences granted to Conferences, upon the condition of accomplishing, so far as in their power, the ordinary works of the Society.   Each one then is stimulated to devote himself to the task; the common Father of the faithful invites us to it, urges us himself to it, and points out to us the way.   Now, if every isolated member, during the leisure of the Vacation, followed this valuable direction, how much good there would result for himself, and for the poor who were about him!   Let us multiply only by two poor people who had received assistance, the number of our brothers who, every year, leave us to settle themselves in the country, or who spend there some months, even some weeks, and we shall be surprised at the blessed harvest which it will be given us to gather in."

He receives every year a report on the works of the Society, and maintains with it a communion both of prayers and good works, by doing whatever works of charity he can, and by advancing the interests of the Society whenever he has an opportunity.

"In a word, is it desired, Sir and dear Brother, that these works, isolated indeed, but which, if my appeal were heard, would not be without their importance, should propagate and last? One precaution is necessary, namely, to maintain between the Society and the corresponding members, constant relations, such as Article 54 of the Rule points out. The BULLETIN of the Society, moreover, affords greater facilities for these relations now than at the commencement of our Conferences; following each of us into his own home, it comes at certain and frequent periods to point out the progress of Conferences, to indicate to us the dangers to shun, the examples to follow, and thus it may contribute to connect with our charitable proceedings the members whom distance separates from us.

"The hope of seeing these members become the most assiduous readers of it, has even been one of the motives to make us undertake this laborious work."

55.—Honorary Members do not assist at the ordinary meetings of the Conferences. They are invited, like the ordinary members, to all other meetings. They are to send every year a special contribution to the Treasurer of the Council or Conference of their town.

As a general rule, the honorary members do not assist at the ordinary meetings of the Conferences; for there would then be cause to ask ourselves why they, taking part in the weekly meetings, should withdraw themselves from the labors of their brothers; yet, whenever they desire to assist at the meetings, it has never been in the spirit of the Society to refuse them admission, since then there is room to hope that they will gain a taste for our works, and will wish to devote themselves to them. But, on the one hand, this cannot be the general rule, and on the other, it is to be remarked that whenever they are admitted to the ordinary meetings, they are not to have a deliberative voice. To act otherwise would often be to leave the decision of questions of grave interest to the Conferences, to persons who are not so versed in all their details, as to possess the spirit of them so well as the active members.

But, if the presence of honorary members at the ordinary meetings of the Conferences be not the Rule, on the contrary their being summoned, as well to the general meetings as to the Masses and pious ceremonies of the Conferences, such as sermons, retreats, etc., is decidedly the rule.

Differently from the active members, who bestow their donations upon their Conferences under the form of secret collections, honorary members are obliged, by force of circumstances, to transmit their offerings in the form of fixed subscriptions. The Rule does not state that their subscription should be the same for every one, nor do the Briefs of Indulgences bear this meaning.

In the towns where there is a Particular Council, the Rule decides that the offering of the honorary members should be handed over to that Council. This is a mode of creating funds for it, and thence establishing among the Conferences a sort of equality for the distribution of aid, notwithstanding the inequality of misery.

The forms of admission are the same for ordinary and honorary members ; when several Conferences are established in a town, honorary members are admitted by the Particular Council.

This point is of very great importance, and unfortunately it is very little observed : at one time honorary members are confounded with subscribers, and no more is required of them than an alms, more or less large, without any consideration being given to their religious habits ; at another time the denomination of "honorary" is given to active members who have been a long time without coming to the Conference, and yet whose names there is some hesitation about erasing. Sometimes even ladies have been enrolled as honorary members. All these customs are contrary to the Rule, and ought to be entirely laid aside; for the honorary members are actually *members of the Society*, according to the terms of the Rule. When they wish to become active members, it is very difficult as a matter of fact, if not perhaps as a matter of right, to refuse it to them; they assist at the feasts, at the Masses, at the general meetings of the Conferences; they are entitled to very extensive Indulgences; whence the consequence is, that to be admitted, they ought to be within the conditions which the Society imposes on its active members; otherwise there would be too great a difference between those two categories of members; and if the one were practical Christians, and the others persons who give little attention to things of a religious character, would there not be reason to fear that in the end the spirit of the Conferences would grow cold as a result of this very dissimilarity, and of the perhaps too great deference which the active members might wish to show towards the honorary members?

Besides the honorary members, there is another category of members which the Rule does not mention, but which the Circular of May 31st, 1846 (*Manual*, page 232), informs us of under the name of members of honor (*membres d'honneur*): they are the clergy who desire to honor the Conferences by the insertion of their names upon our roll, and whom it seems to be much more respectful to designate under the title of members of honor (*membres d'honneur*), than under that of *honorary members*.

56.—Every Conference may have, moreover, simple subscribers—these are not members of the Society, but are entitled as benefactors to its prayers.

This article diminishes the last objections which might remain against the decision of the preceding article upon the conditions required for honorary members; for it points out the modes of making useful to the poor the generosity of those persons, men or women, who wish to bestow their alms upon the Conferences, and who, either because they do not fulfil the religious conditions, or by reason of their sex, cannot, according to the Rule, be admitted as honorary members. Subscribers, not being members of the Society, can be received from among persons of every religious opinion, and this latitude cannot lead to any inconvenience.

Many Conferences turn to use, in a way which is very profitable to the poor, the zeal of lady-benefactresses, either as collectors, or for the wardrobe, or the employment of the poor, or for some works with which the Conferences cannot engage themselves in a direct manner. Such zeal deserves to be imitated.

CHAPTER VI.

THE FESTIVALS OF THE SOCIETY.

57.—The Society celebrates the Feast of the Immaculate Conception of the Blessed Virgin and the Feast of St. Vincent de Paul, its patron. The Conferences assist in a body at Mass, on the 8th of December and 19th of July, and also on the anniversary of the translation of the relics of St. Vincent de Paul.

According to the Brief of January 10th, 1845, the festivals should be celebrated on the very day of the Immaculate Conception of the Blessed Virgin, the 8th of December, and on that of the Feast of St. Vincent de Paul, the 19th of July. If the day were changed, the Indulgences could no longer be obtained. As actual difficulties often arose, as to Conferences, and particularly those in the country, fulfilling these conditions, the result unhappily was that a great number of Conferences were deprived of the Indulgences which the Common Father of the Faithful has dispensed to us with so great liberality. To rem-

edy this inconvenience, the Council-General has solicited
of the Sovereign Pontiff a modification of the Brief of the
10th of January, 1845, and the extension of these precious
favors, which it has obtaified by a third Brief, bearing
date the 18th of March, 1853, is as follows:

1st. The Plenary Indulgences granted by the Brief of
the 10th of January, 1845, for the 8th of December, can
be obtained at the Masses specially celebrated for the Society, either on the very day of the Feast of the Immaculate Conception, or on the day to which it is transferred in
the diocese.

2d. The Plenary Indulgence granted by the Brief of
the 10th of January, 1845, for the Feast of St. Vincent de
Paul, can be obtained, either on the 19th of July, or during the seven days which follow it.

3d. At Paris, the Indulgence for the Feast of St. Vincent de Paul can be obtained at the Masses of the Laza-
rist Fathers, even if it be not celebrated for the Society.

On these days the members pray for the prosperity of the Catholic Church, for the increase
of charity among men, and to draw down the
blessings of God on the work in which they are
associated. Should any member be absent from
the locality, or otherwise prevented from attending, he assists in spirit at least with his brethren,
and prays for them as they pray for him.

The observance of the festivals of the Society is one of
the obligations with which we ought to be most deeply
impressed. How, in fact, can the members of Conferences
hope to see their labors prosper, if they do not go to beseech God to bless them, and what more powerful means
of obtaining this blessing is there, than to ask it all in
common, united by the same prayer and the same faith, at
the foot of the same altars? Besides, how is it possible to
make up for the union of hearts, which is the result of
these pious practices and one of their most precious re
sults? Without the festivals of the Society, the ties which
mutually bind the Conferences together would be very
quickly loosened, and the material means which have been

pointed out many times already would soon become useless for the want of spiritual means, those blessed by the
Church. It is, therefore, of the very highest importance
that every Conference, and that in every Conference every
member, observe the four festivals of the Society as scrupulously as is possible; for we are not afraid of asserting
that a member, however zealous, however Christian-like
he may in other respects be, does not possess the true
spirit of the Society, if he voluntarily neglect to observe
its feasts, and that a Conference which falls into this
danger sees in a short time the spirit of St. Vincent de
Paul grow weaker, and become extinct within it.

58.—The day after the general meeting in
Lent, all the members of the Society assist in a
body at the *Requiem* Mass, which is offered in
the town for the repose of the souls of the deceased members of the Society.

The religious care of the dead is one of the conditions
of the existence of a lasting work, and in Christianity it is
so rigorous a duty, that to omit it is in some sort to fail
in one of the principal obligations of the Christian life.
Accordingly the Rule has expressly recommended it; and
accordingly the usage has since been established, over and
above, of reciting during the meeting of the Conference,
the *De profundis* for the members lately deceased, and of
having Mass celebrated for the repose of their souls.
Some Conferences, not content with the anniversary of
the first Monday in Lent, add to it that of the Commem-
oration of the dead. The Brief of the 10th of January,
1845, recompenses by a special Indulgence the act of
assisting at Masses for the deceased members.

OBSERVATION.

59.—None of the preceding rules impose an
obligation of conscience, but the Society relies
for their fulfilment on the zeal of its members,
and their love of God and their neighbors.

REGULATIONS

FOR THE

UPPER COUNCILS.

(Extract from the *Bulletin* of the 1st of May, 1850.)

For many years the really providential spread of the Society has, in the countries situated outside France, rendered an institution necessary which our first rules did not anticipate, namely, that of Councils charged with the direction of the Conferences of an entire country, and constituted as intermediate between the Council-General, the centre of all the Society, and the Conferences separated from it by distance, language, and local customs.

This institution, self-begotten, so to speak, has become happily extended, and has contributed, by its development, to the progress of our work in foreign countries, where otherwise it would have penetrated with difficulty, and where particularly it would have sustained itself with still greater difficulty. In their turn, England, Ireland, Belgium, Holland, Rhenish Prussia, Silesia, Mexico, Canada, have seen such Councils established within their bosom; and as a result of this organization, the Conferences of these different countries have been formed with greater facility in a common spirit, and have been multiplied in a more rapid manner. Experience was then conclusive, and the moment was come for incorporating into our written rules a collection of regulations applicable to these Councils: these form arrangements which, without infringing upon usages already venerable in some portions of the Society, and confirmed moreover by the Council-General, without being even a code, invariable and absolute for the future, yet may serve as a guide and as a model for Councils as they are successively formed.

With this idea the Council-General has drawn up a series of articles in addition to the Rule; but before adopt-

7

ing them in a definitive manner, it desired to receive information from the good advice of the Councils of Europe,
that is to say, of those which time and distance allowed it
to consult. This advice did not fail the Council-General,
to whom it has been most valuable; it has most certainly
contributed to improve so important a Rule.

The regulations which we are about to explain briefly,
and the text of which we give further on, form a summary
of the local usages, and of the chapters of the General
Rule relative to Particular Councils and to the Council-
General itself. These Councils are, in fact, intermediate
between the Particular Councils of a town, charged with
the interests of Conferences of a city, and the Council-
General, charged with the direction of all the Conferences.
Their functions, as their nature, ought then to possess
something mutual, and this idea has been uppermost in
the preparation of the rules respecting them.

At the very commencement, a primary question arose,
as to the name to be given to these Councils. Should
they be designated in the Rule, under the title of Provin-
cial Councils, as the two Briefs of the 10th of February
and 12th of August, 1845, had done? Powerful reasons
weighed in favor of this expression, one already old among
us, and accepted by most of the Councils; but the appre-
hension which was manifested, that in many countries it
would awaken national susceptibilities dangerous to the
Society, has induced us to adopt a new denomination—
that of Upper Councils.

The circumscription of the Upper Councils, and the lo-
cation of their seat, are points which the first Article of
this Rule hands over to the Council-General, by virtue of
the delegation which it makes to them of a part of its
own rights. It is the practice, converted purely and simply into a written rule.

The 8d Article treats of an important question, that of
the constitution itself of the Upper Council. After having
well considered it, and weighed the different opinions expressed, it has been judged preferable to summon all the
Conferences (whom the Upper Council is to unite) to co-
operate in its formation, in order thereby to make its
authority greater. This co-operation may take place,
either by means of delegates, chosen in equal numbers by
each Conference, or by means of correspondence, accord-

ing to local circumstances; and finally, it is sufficient for the validity of the constitution of the Council, that all the Conferences should be *summoned* to take part in it: it is not necessary that they should actually have done so, if they neglect to reply to the Convocation. To establish greater order, the election should be directed by the Particular Council established in the town where the Upper Council is to have its seat, or by the Conference of that town, if a Particular Council is not as yet in existence.

The 4th Article reproduces for the nomination of the President of the Upper Council, a mode which is analogous to that adopted for the nomination of the President-General, and which experience has shown the advantages of. But the delay of two months is reduced to one month, as the circumscription is less extended.

The 8th Article anticipates the case where there are in the same town an Upper Council and a Particular Council. In such a case it is decided that the presidentship of the Particular Council belongs of right to the President of the Upper Council; but the latter may delegate it if he believe it necessary. This point has been already settled by the General Rule as to Paris, where both the Council General and the Particular Council of the town assemble, and it has been sanctioned by fifteen years' experience. It has, then, appeared to be useful to extend it here to the cases in which multiplicity of affairs, or any other reason, would prevent, as in many towns, the functions of the Particular Council being intrusted to the Upper Council.

The 10th Article affirms the unvarying judicial powers of the Council-General, relative to the admission of Conferences into our Society. It is for the Council-General to pronounce upon their aggregation, having, however, taken the advice of the Upper Councils.

This mode, while preserving the common spirit—the unity which is indispensable—associates the Local Councils in the development of our charitable family; it provides against the diversity of regulations—it consolidates our little, our wholly fraternal plan of government, while preventing the admission, without cause shown, of new Conferences who come to ask the rights of fellowship among us.

These happy relations of fraternity and of union are still more closely cemented by the 12th Article, which, by summoning the Presidents of Upper Councils into the bosom of the Council-General, by giving them the right to take their places there, when they are at Paris, by suggesting that when they are absent, their advice upon grave questions by means of written communications, be taken, assures thus to the whole Society the concurrence of their intelligence, their devotion, and of their charity. The first trial, which has been made of it in anticipation in the drawing up of the present Rule, has already sufficiently proved it in the eyes of the Council-General.

Let us conclude by two observations:

1st. The articles which are about to be perused form henceforth part of the General Rule; they have been inserted in it; but it has appeared preferable not to blend them into the body of the Rule itself, and not to derange the order, now an old one, of the articles; to touch it, would have been to introduce disagreeable confusion, and to alter in some degree a record venerated in our Society, since it is almost contemporaneous with its foundation. Moreover, the authority of these new arrangements will not, on this account, be less in the eyes of our Conferences and of all our brothers.

2d. The present Rule is applicable to Councils now existing abroad, whose mission it is to direct the Conferences belonging to distinct nations. But it is not, and it has not been, an obstacle to the formation of Councils of a more limited circumscription, which have become, and are daily becoming, more necessary for binding closely together among themselves the Conferences which are situated near one another. Far from it: it is for such Conferences a model and a basis for organization.

The following, then, is the text of this Rule, adopted by the Council-General at its meeting of the 1st of April, 1850:

Art. 1.—When the Conferences of a more extensive circumscription than that of a Particular Council, desire to be united by a Council, an Upper Council may be constituted for this purpose, conformably to the terms of the Brief of our Holy Father, Pope Gregory XVI., dated

January the 10th, 1845. This Council is named after the circumscription for which it is established, and which is determined by the Council-General; its seat is fixed by the Council-General.

This Council, within its circumscription, is the representative of the General Council, which forms the centre of the whole Brotherhood, and it governs all the Councils and Conferences already established, or which may be established there. Its object is to preserve the unity and spirit of the Brotherhood there; it forms the natural and usual link of correspondence between the Councils and Conferences with the General Council.

2.—The Upper Council consists of a President, of one or more Vice-Presidents, of a Secretary, a Treasurer, one or several Vice-Secretaries, a Vice-Treasurer, and of several Councillors.

3.—When the President is to be named for the first time, all the Conferences of the circumscription are invited to assist in doing so. The election shall take place under the superintendence of the Conference or Council belonging to the town wherein the Upper Council is to be established.

4.—When a new President is to be named, the Vice-President assembles the Council. This preparatory sitting is devoted to deliberation as to who may be an eligible person for this office. If the former President be still alive, he is in-

7*

vited to designate the person whom he would deem it of advantage to select.

When the members have come to an understanding upon one or several names, the meeting adjourns for a month: during the interval the proceedings of this preparatory meeting are made known to the Presidents of the Particular Councils, who consult their colleagues, and to the Presidents of the Conferences, who consult their respective Councils, or even the Conferences over which they preside; all the Presidents transmit their opinions to the Council, and according to these opinions the Council makes the election; an exact minute of which is recorded.

While the election is pending, all the members of the circumscription address, either in private or at the meetings, a special prayer to God, such as the *Veni Creator*, in order that His Spirit may guide them throughout the intended election.

5.—The members of the Upper Council are named, as well of those of the Board, by the President, with the advice of the Council.

6.—The President presides over the Upper Council, and over the general meetings of the Conferences of the town where it is established. He convenes extraordinary meetings. In case of absence, his place is supplied by the Vice-President, or even, if necessary, by any other member of the Council.

7.—The Secretary keeps an account of the

names, Christian names, professions, residences, and dates of reception of the different members of the Conferences belonging to the town where the Upper Council holds its sittings. He also notes down the persons who form the Boards of the Councils, or of the Conferences of the circumscription, as well as the places where, and days and hours when, they hold their sittings.

He draws up the minutes of the sittings held by the Council and general meetings; prepares the annual report upon the works of the Conferences of the circumscription, and transmits it to the General Council. He is intrusted, under the superintendence of the President, with the general correspondence that is kept up with the Presidents and Secretaries of the Councils and Conferences, as well as with the General Council. He has the custody of the records of the Society in that circumscription.

The Treasurer has the care of the funds. He keeps an exact account of the receipts and expenditure; he submits his accounts to the Council.

8.—In case the Upper Council does not fulfil, for the local Conferences, the office of a Particular Council, the presidency of the latter devolves by right on the President of the Upper Council, who names the Presidents and Vice-Presidents of the Conferences and Special Works, as also the Board of the Particular Council.

In case of any impediment, his presidency

over the Particular Council is supplied by a member of the Upper Council, whom he delegates for that purpose.

9.—The funds of the Council are maintained by extraordinary donations made to the Society, by collections at the General Meetings of the town in which it is established, and by the contributions which are annually sent by each Conference, or by each Council of the circumscription, towards the general expenses.

10.—When a Conference or Particular Council is about to be formed in the circumscription, the Upper Council examines how far it may be proper to propose its aggregation to the General Council. This aggregation can never take place but with the previous advice of the Upper Council.

It likewise refers to the General Council, when it is deemed necessary to dissolve any particular Conference or Council. In a case of urgency, it may temporarily suspend the sittings, and refer the matter to the General Council.

11.—The Upper Council governs all the practical details of the Conferences in the circumscription, either through the medium of correspondence or of circulars from the President, and watches over the observance of the Rules, reserving, however, to the General Council weighty questions, and such as may concern the welfare of the Society at large.

12.—The Presidents of the Upper Councils,

when present in Paris, attend at and take part
in the sittings of the General Council, of which
they are members, as long as they continue to
fill the same office.

The General Council may ask for their opinion
in writing upon such matters as interest the
whole Brotherhood.

INDEX.

Accounts of Conferences should be verified yearly, 25.

Admission of Candidates, how to be announced, 27.

Adoption of families, for relief, 86, 87.

Aggregation, how to be solicited, 11 ; necessary for participation in the Indulgences, 12 ; powers of Upper Councils as to, 75, 80.

Aspirant Members, 64.

Benefactresses, ladies may be, 8.

Books for persons relieved, 25, 35.

Candidates for admission as Members, 27–30.

Certificates of Membership, as to, 31.

Charity, no work of, foreign to the Society, 9, 10.

Clergy, preside at General Meetings, 68 ; are members of honor (*membres d'honneur*), 69.

Clothing for the poor, 25 ; grants of, 35.

Collections, at the meetings of Conferences, 40 ; purpose of, 41.

Conferences, intended for men only, 7 ; aim of, is zeal for the salvation of souls, 8 ; what, 11 ; how admitted to aggregation, 11, 80 ; powers of Upper Councils relative to admission of, into the Society, 75 ; how named, *id.* ; united by a Council-General, 12 ; meetings of, 14 ; should correspond with each other, 15, 16 ; should give attention to soldiers, 17 ; organization of, *id.* ; Council of, how constituted, *id.* ; officers of, how nominated, 18, 19 ; duties of President, 21 ; when President of Upper Council has power to name President, 79 ; duties of Secretary, 22 ; of Treasurer, 24 ; of Librarian, 25 ; funds of, 24, 81 ; wardrobe of, 25 ; prayers at, 26 ; relief tickets, how distributed, 32 ; deliberations of, on plans for relief of the distressed, 36 ; members leaving, 38 ; *special works*, reports of, when to be read, 40 ; collection, when made, *id.* ; when several established in same town, 43 ; how represented in Particular Council, 51 ; poorer Conferences, how assisted by Particular Council, 47 ; by Council-General, 54 ; General Meetings of, 59 ; may have subscribers, 69 ; contributions of, to Upper Councils, 80 ; dissolution or suspension of, *id.* ; corresponding members, 64–67.

www.ingramcontent.com/pod-product-compliance
Lightning Source LLC
Chambersburg PA
CBHW020546270326
41927CB00006B/742